For the Love of CUB SCOUTS

*The unofficial guide for building
a stronger pack—your Scouts will
love—in only an hour a week*

Wm. David Levesque

"This is not an official publication of the BSA
and is not approved or endorsed by the BSA"

authorHOUSE®

AuthorHouse™
1663 Liberty Drive
Bloomington, IN 47403
www.authorhouse.com
Phone: 1-800-839-8640

This is not an official BSA publication and the BSA is not responsible for its content.

Arrow of Light™, Boy Scout™, Boy Scouts of America®, Boys' Life®, BSA®, Cub Scout™, Cub Scouts®, Do Your Best™, Eagle Scout™, Good Turn for America®, Order of the Arrow®, Pinewood Derby®, Raingutter Regatta ™, Scouting®, Scoutmaster®, Scout Shop®, Scout Stuff®, Space Derby®, Venture®, Venturing®, Wood Badge®, Boy Scout, Cub Scout and Venturing mottoes and phrases, Boy Scout uniform, insignia and emblems, Cub Scout uniform, insignia and emblems are trademarks of the Boy Scouts of America. Marks contained herein are used with permission. All rights reserved.

Published by AuthorHouse 8/6/2013

ISBN: 978-1-4918-0540-4 (sc)
ISBN: 978-1-4918-0539-8 (e)

Library of Congress Control Number: 2013913760

Any people depicted in stock imagery provided by Thinkstock are models, and such images are being used for illustrative purposes only. Certain stock imagery © Thinkstock.

This book is printed on acid-free paper.

Table of Contents

To Josh—I dedicate this book to my favorite Cub Scout.
To Caitlin, Kyle and Claire—I wish we could have shared Scouting too.

Love, Dad

To Jeanette—who loved <u>me</u> so much, she shared my Scouting journey

Love, Dave

Josh as a Tiger Cub

After Baden-Powell's death, a letter was found in his desk that he had written to all Scouts. It included this passage: "Try and leave this world a little better than you found it."

Foreword

Congratulations! I'm assuming the reason you have selected this book is because you would like to help make the Cub Scout program stronger in your pack. Perhaps you are a new Cubmaster, committee chair or den leader? Possibly, you have recently been asked to serve as a charter organization representative. You might be a parent who wants to know how to make your son's Cub Scout pack experience as fun and fulfilling as possible. Whatever your reason, I want to thank you for your desire to make Scouting better.

It has been my experience that the formal training developed by the Boy Scouts of America and delivered locally through the various councils is very well designed and enthusiastically delivered. What I came to learn, as a new Cubmaster, was there was further information I wanted (or needed) that was not contained in the formal training.

My goal in creating this book is to provide a little bit more of that same "further information" for the next generation of Cub Scout pack leaders. I will do my best to make the topics flow easily, without unnecessarily repeating what you will already learn through the formal training available.

I entered Cub Scouts as the parent of a 1st grader. My son, Josh, told my wife and I that someone came to school that day to tell the boys all about Cub Scouts. There was a meeting scheduled for that evening for those families that might like more information about how to join. The rest is history...

I was in Boy Scouts as a youth, but never in Cub Scouts. In addition to earning First Class rank, I completed a religious emblem for my faith, attended junior leadership training and was inducted into the Order of the Arrow (I may be the longest tenured active Ordeal Arrowman).

I have always felt that my Boy Scout experiences and training have played an important role towards my adult achievements. I also learned that Scouting as I knew it (or remembered it) as a Boy Scout is different than how Scouting is delivered in Cub Scouts. There was much to learn—and some to unlearn.

One of the most impressive aspects of Scouting is the incredible spirit of helpfulness and fellowship exhibited by volunteers. When you consider how many topics can bring polarizing passions between adults (politics, religion, culture, sports, race, gender, ...) it is a wonder how Scouting volunteers seem quite capable to check those differences at the door and stay focused on what binds us together in order to deliver the best Scouting program for our youth that we can.

I can promise you this, should you ever ask for help when amongst Scouting volunteers—you will surely receive an enthusiastic response. As you progress in your new Scouting role (or any future Scouting role), whatever that role, this statement should be of comfort and assistance for you to remember.

This publication dives a little deeper into some topics I believe you will find to be important as you focus on delivering stronger program for your pack. While it is possible for Scouting roles to become overwhelming and time consuming—this is not necessary in order to do it well. I will share some techniques that will help you build a program with your Scouts, that they will find to be exciting and fun, your families will find fulfilling and that you will find you can do without losing your mind.

Scouting volunteers (Scouters) and Scouting professionals alike, love to freely share ideas that they have found to be useful—in a genuine intention of making Scouting better. A challenge many Scouters may experience is accurately identifying the source of an approach or a story in order to provide deserved credit. This is further challenged by over 100 years of Scouting, where even what may seem to be a new idea—just might be an old idea coming around again for the first time. My objective in writing this book was not to take specific credit for any innovation or the creativeness of an idea, but rather to collect as much pragmatic advice as might be practical to share so that you could build a stronger pack—your Scouts will love—in only an hour a week.

My Scouting journey has been blessed by the fellowship and guidance of so many incredible volunteers and professionals. My pack experience was the result of an extraordinary team of volunteers. My heartfelt thanks to Eric Wolf, Andy Thompson, Mike Bailey, Todd Weihoneig, Rob Keister, and Harold Smith—for all they did to make our sons' Scouting experience memorable.

It would be challenging to attempt to take on a leader role in Scouting without creating any impact at home. My wife, Jeanette, actively encouraged me to be our son's Tiger Cub parent when Josh wanted to join the pack. As a former Boy Scout, I felt I could be a resource to the pack—but I did not contemplate a formal role as a pack leader. It soon became obvious that a new Cubmaster would be needed. As my focus on building a stronger pack deepened, so did the support and assistance I received from Jeanette. For me, it was moving testimony of her love for Josh and I—since she freely loaned her highly capable organizing and people skills—ultimately serving as pack committee chair. She made us a great team. It always pays to marry up.

At a district level, I received tremendous guidance and counsel from so many experienced Scouters. I would like to mention a few of them that played a particularly impactful role in my development: Lorry Wisse, Peter Reeb, Jim Gagnon, Val Kalwas, Dan Scurlock, Craig Royce, Mary Royce and my personal Scouting mentor—Charles Arnold. Now or in the future—Silver Beavers all.

By accident of location, I found myself a member of the Seneca Waterways Council. There is no finer council in the land. Prior and current leadership has left for our Scouts and Scouters a legacy of the best that Scouting has to offer. It is no small wonder considering the contributions of volunteers like Craig Kaplan, Jim Roth, David Finger and David Lippitt. A vital component to the council's success has been the leadership talent, drive and collaborative spirit extended to volunteers by the professional staff. Much of this credit goes to Scout Executive Stephen Hoitt, Director of Field Services Gary Decker and (in my district) District Executive Adam Cregg. They come to work every day committed to deliver Scouting's best to our community. The council and district track records for earning gold level Journey to Excellence awards testify to their effectiveness.

Seneca Waterways Council has made a bold statement regarding their commitment to Scouting's future through their sizeable investment in developing one of the premier Cub Scout Activity Camps in the nation. As your pack considers possible outdoor adventures and camping experiences to add to your annual pack program plan—you owe it to your Scouts and their families to consider utilizing the Camp Cutler Reservation, located near Naples, New York. If you would like see a brief video highlighting what the Cub Adventure Camp offers, you can find some videos that my son Josh and I put together on YouTube. These venues (and others) are available year round. Search for:

- Camp Cutler—Fort Radcliff
- Camp Cutler—Eastman Castle

I have heard it said that a book that is not read is not worth the paper it is written on. I suspect this is true. I have attempted to include content that you will find valuable towards building a stronger pack—your Scouts will love—in only an hour a week. My challenge was to include enough content to make the book a value to the reader, while not making it so large that it might become intimidating to use. Might I suggest that if your busy schedule makes it necessary, tear out a few pages from the book every day and read them as your time allows. A terrific looking book, left unread on the shelf, will be of little benefit—whereas a totally consumed book, whose contents are placed into action might actually be found to be priceless. I hope your Scouts will think so...

In closing, I thank you for your service to Scouting. I also thank you for investing in this book, since it demonstrates your desire and commitment to make Scouting better for your Scouts and Scout families.

I will be directing any profits I may receive from the sale of this book back into Scouting. I hope this will give you another reason to feel good about your purchase.

Author and son
Not an official BSA publication and the BSA is not responsible for its content

Chapter 1

Cub Scout Program Basics

The material in this chapter comes directly from leader training materials (Cub Scout Leader Handbook and Scouting.org) developed by the Boy Scouts of America (BSA). While my aim is to avoid repeating materials you will receive through formal training—I have learned to value these materials as useful guideposts and references for building a strong and vibrant pack.

The Aim of Scouting

The overall mission of the Boy Scouts of America is to help youth build character, learn citizenship, and develop personal fitness.

The 10 Purposes of Cub Scouts:

Character Development   Spiritual Growth
Good Citizenship   Sportsmanship and Fitness
Family Understanding   Respectful Relationships
Personal Achievement   Friendly Service
Fun and Adventure   Preparation for Boy Scouts

Every Cub Scouting activity should help fulfill one of these purposes. When considering a new activity, ask which purpose or purposes it supports. Not everything in Cub Scouting has to be serious—far from it! Silly songs, energetic games, and fun to make snacks all have their place in the program. Keep in mind that a necessary ingredient of keeping Scouting attractive to boys is that they need to have fun while they are doing it. It's not a bad goal for adult volunteers either. If you're not having some fun—you are doing it wrong. When in doubt on this, ask your unit commissioner for some helpful advice.

Cub Scouting's 12 Core Values

1. **Citizenship**—Contributing service and showing responsibility to local, state, and national communities.
2. **Compassion**—Being kind and considerate and showing concern for the well-being of others.
3. **Cooperation**—Being helpful and working together with others toward a common goal.
4. **Courage**—Being brave and doing what is right regardless of our fears, the difficulties, or the consequences.
5. **Faith**—Having inner strength and confidence based on our trust in God.
6. **Health and Fitness**—Being personally committed to keeping our minds and bodies clean and fit.
7. **Honesty**—Telling the truth and being worthy of trust.
8. **Perseverance**—Sticking with something and not giving up, even if it is difficult.
9. **Positive Attitude**—Being cheerful and setting our minds to look for and find the best in all situations.
10. **Resourcefulness**—Using human and other resources to their fullest.
11. **Respect**—Showing regard for the worth of something or someone.
12. **Responsibility**—Fulfilling our duty to God, country, other people, and ourselves.

Character can be defined as the collection of core values by an individual that leads to moral commitment and action. Character development should challenge Cub Scouts to experience core values in six general areas: God, world, country, community, family, and self. As you plan your annual pack program—ask yourself if the activities and events you plan touch on these aspects.

The Methods of Cub Scouting

To accomplish its purposes and achieve the overall goals of building character, learning citizenship, and developing personal fitness, Cub Scouting uses seven methods:

1. **Living the Ideals**

   Cub Scouting's values are embedded in the <u>Cub Scout Promise,</u> the <u>Law of the Pack</u>, the Cub Scout <u>motto</u>, and the Cub Scout <u>sign</u>, <u>handshake</u>, and <u>salute</u>. These practices help establish and reinforce the program's values in boys and the leaders who guide them.

2. **Belonging to a Den**

   The den—a group of six to eight boys who are about the same age—is the place where Cub Scouting starts. In the den, Cub Scouts develop new skills and interests, they practice sportsmanship and good citizenship, and they learn to do their best, not just for themselves but for the den as well.

3. **Using Advancement**

   Recognition is important to boys. The advancement plan provides fun for the boys, gives them a sense of personal achievement as they earn badges, and strengthens family understanding as adult family members and their den leader work with boys on advancement projects.

4. **Involving Family and Home**

   Whether a Cub Scout lives with two parents or one, a foster family, or other relatives, his family is an important part of Cub Scouting. Parents and adult family members provide leadership and support for Cub Scouting and help ensure that boys have a good experience in the program.

5. **Participating in Activities**

   Cub Scouts participate in a huge array of activities, including games, projects, skits, stunts, songs, outdoor activities, trips and service projects. Besides being fun, these activities offer opportunities for growth, achievement, and family involvement.

6. **Serving Home and Neighborhood**
    Cub Scouting focuses on the home and neighborhood. It helps boys strengthen connections to their local communities, which in turn support the boys' growth and development.

7. **Wearing the Uniform**
    Cub Scout uniforms serve a dual purpose, demonstrating membership in the group (everyone is dressed alike) and individual achievement (boys wear the badges they've earned). Wearing the uniform to meetings and activities also encourages a neat appearance, a sense of belonging, and good behavior.

8. **Making Character Connections**
    Throughout the program, leaders learn to identify and use character lessons in activities so boys can learn to know, commit, and practice the 12 core values of Cub Scouting. Character Connections are included in all the methods of Cub Scouting and are the program themes for monthly pack meetings.

The Cub Scout Promise

I promise to do my best, to do my duty to God and my country, to help other people, and to obey the Law of the Pack.

The Law of the Pack

The Cub Scout follows Akela, the Cub Scout helps the Pack go, the Pack helps the Cub Scout grow, the Cub Scout gives goodwill.

Cub Scout Motto "Do Your Best"

This is an excellent motto to keep in mind as a Scout pack volunteer—both in regards to the efforts of young Scouts, as well as well-meaning volunteers. Commit it to memory...

I have included the Scout Oath and Scout Law for two reasons. At the time of this writing there is talk of consolidating Cub Scouts, Boy Scouts and Venturing under a common Scout Oath by January 1, 2014. Secondly, since one of the principle objectives of Cub Scouts is to prepare boys for Boy Scouts—you may as well become familiar with it.

The Scout Oath
On my honor I will do my best
To do my duty to God and my country
and to obey the Scout Law;
To help other people at all times;
To keep myself physically strong,
mentally awake, and morally straight.

The Scout Law
A Scout is:

Trustworthy	Loyal	Helpful
Friendly	Courteous	Kind
Obedient	Cheerful	Thrifty
Brave	Clean	Reverent

When in doubt about behavior or intentions, ask yourself if it is consistent with the 12 Scout Laws. It is a bright star to guide your voyage upon a dark night.

The Boy Scouts of America maintains that no member can grow into the best kind of citizen without recognizing an obligation to God and, therefore, recognizes the religious element in the training of the member, but it is absolutely nonsectarian in its attitude toward that religious training. Scouting encourages a Scout to recognize an obligation or duty to God, but does not define what a belief in God is or define what constitutes a religious organization. As Scout leaders we must be careful not to favor one faith over another. In conducting Scouting activities, we must be sensitive to the need to encourage all Scouts to grow in their own religious beliefs and faiths. Remember that Scouts have a "Duty to God."

Chapter 2

Pack Structure

At the risk of repeating materials presented in leader specific training—I would like to invest a chapter towards better understanding pack structure.

Many packs suffer from a lack of understanding of how a pack should be structured. This can lead to two types of outcomes:

1. Role confusion which leads to weak program design, poor program delivery, and ultimately stagnation.
2. Failure to differentiate that there are many roles within the pack—so while it is clear what is to be done, there is too much for each available leader to reasonably do.

Both outcomes can be avoided.

For those reading this book who feel they possess a strong command of the different roles of pack leaders, but simply lack sufficient volunteers to do the work—take heart, I will address this issue in an upcoming chapter.

On a bigger picture scale, it is by no accident that unit structure is essentially the same across all programs and levels of Scouting (Cub Scouts, Boy Scouts, Venturing, districts, councils, areas, regions and at national). For each of these programs or levels of Scouting there is program, membership, and finance. You will also find commissioning service throughout Scouting, providing counsel and access to assistance in order to deliver stronger program. It is what commissioners do.

Within program, membership, and finance there can be a multiple of sub-categories.

- Program: advancement, recognition, training, camp promotion, community service, etc...
- Membership: recruitment, retention, etc...
- Finance: budget, fund raising, Friends of Scouting (FOS), inventory, etc...

Great theory and foundation, but let's explore how all this applies to your pack.

All Scouting units belong to a chartered organization, which is any organization that agrees to sponsor a Scouting unit in collaboration with a local Scout council. Each chartered organization has an institutional head that selects a chartered organization representative (COR), who works directly with the pack. Through the COR, the chartered organization selects and approves the Scout leader volunteers who serve the pack. The COR also works with the pack committee to make sure the pack delivers program consistent with the standards of the B.S.A. and complimentary with the objectives of the chartered organization.

The pack committee chair is responsible for organizing the pack committee and ensuring the successful execution of:

- Collaborative relationship with the chartered organization
- Support of the policies of the B.S.A.
- Creation and periodic review of pack policy
- Positive Scouting relationships within the community
- Annual pack program plan
- Creation of a pack budget
- Funding

- Delivery of pack program and advancement
- Camping promotion
- Community service
- Advancement record-keeping
- Timely payment of pack bills
- Recruitment of Scouts
- Recruitment and training for volunteers
- Timely and accurate re-chartering
- Creation and distribution of meeting agendas and notes
- Maintaining productive relationships with area troops
- Ensuring a smooth transition of Webelos Scouts into troops

In healthy, vibrant packs, these responsibilities are deployed through several adult volunteers who are a part of the pack committee. Often-times, this work is completed by only one or two high-energy, high-passion volunteers. When this is the case, any early success with this model of leadership is often doomed to eventual failure and pack stagnation. The effort either becomes too much for a leader to sustain and they burnout—or—when it is time for them to transition to another role in Scouting, there is nobody available who is capable (or willing) to take on the full scope of this work. The problem is that if this is the only model of leadership that a pack knows—they will fail to find a new leader and eventually struggle to re-charter. This scenario, which can occur too often, is quite avoidable. The key is to distribute the role of the pack committee across a multiple of adult volunteers so that "many hands make light work."

So, clearly a committee of three must assume personal responsibility for more areas than a committee of seven or more. History has shown that a larger committee typically results in a stronger, consistent pack that can more effectively deliver quality program. A larger committee also means a larger percentage of families are involved and committed towards the success of the pack. All around it is a win-win formula.

A strong pack committee will have individual members assigned to such areas as: record keeping, finances, fund raising, advancement, event planning, training, public relations, membership and re-chartering. It is the pack committee chair's role to prepare, recruit, assign, train and recognize volunteers to serve the needs of the committee.

In my opinion, the glue for the pack is successful dens. If dens are meeting, having fun and earning regular advancement—you will not only have productive den meetings, you will have full, high energy pack meetings as well. If attendance and advancement stall in your dens, a vibrant pack will become unsustainable. A key to success, in my mind, is properly supporting your den leaders.

Quite often, a leader for one rank will volunteer to remain the den leader for the following rank. This tends to build a strong sense of team and belonging within that den. As a Cubmaster, I recognized the critical nature of the den leader's role early. I always tried to have at least two trained den leaders per rank so if life got in the way for one leader, the other leader could keep things progressing along. Our pack always made it a point to get our new leaders (or current leaders taking on a new role) trained as quickly as possible. This went a long way towards increasing their comfort level in taking on the task at hand. I also found many den leaders felt more comfortable volunteering if they knew there was another den leader to share the journey.

In addition to formally trained den leaders, we recruited other den adults into "part-time" leader roles. Since most pack families join when their boys are Tiger Cubs, many den adults are already familiar with the concept of "sponsoring" a den meeting along with the Tiger Cub den leader. We simply leveraged this idea beyond Tiger Cubs.

Early in the start of the new pack year, we gathered all the adults of the den around the table and shared with them the den meeting plans. These are typically 1-2 page summaries that describe the preparation for, flow and wrap-up for a den meeting. They can be purchased inexpensively at your Scout Store or online at ScoutStuff.org. They can also be downloaded from Scouting.org for free. By selecting and sequencing these den meeting plans, a den can plan out their entire year—including developing a budget. This makes it easier to find den leaders, it facilitates getting adults to volunteer to help in a meeting or two throughout the year and most importantly it helps you to build a stronger pack—your Scouts will love—in only one hour a week. More on how to do this in our chapter on volunteers.

Your Cubmaster focuses on delivering specific program objectives at pack and den meetings and guides the den leaders. The Cubmaster also serves as the emcee for the pack meetings. Whenever possible, avoid the temptation to assign further duties to your den leaders and Cubmaster.

All too often, packs fail to effectively recruit adults from their pack families to fill key roles in membership and finance. Failing to do so can overload your den leaders, Cubmaster and committee chair. These volunteers already have a full plate with regular deliverables. By also giving them membership and finance duties to fill—their time requirements to the pack will skyrocket. This is not only unfair, it is often unsustainable. If your pack is presently in this predicament, make a commitment amongst your pack leadership to get this situation turned around within this very pack year. I'll share some ideas on how to turn this around in the chapter on volunteers.

Your membership chair can focus on planning and executing effective recruiting events in order to offer to more boys in your area the promise of Scouting. They can also lead efforts to facilitate successful transition of your Webelos Scouts into area troops. Of course, nothing prevents your membership chair from drafting the assistance from other adults in the pack. Your best shot at growing membership is to have a focused plan that is well executed. Your best shot at productive results is if this task is adopted by someone who can provide it dedicated attention and energy. Some packs have experienced some challenges growing their membership, but I have some exciting and positive news to share on this topic. This is so important to your pack's success and your Scouts positive attitude about Scouting that we will devote an entire chapter to the topic a bit later on.

Your finance chair can take the lead in providing a budget to deliver your intended program for the year. They can also help coordinate your fund raising efforts, as well as perform any bookkeeping. Recruit other adults as necessary to meet the demands of these roles.

Many packs also have pack trainers. This is a terrific role for a more seasoned Cub Scout leader to fill. As with many roles in Scouting, there is formal training to help guide them on how to fill this role.

Based on the Family Talent Survey (an example of a survey follows in the next chapter) that you collected from Scout families, you may find several adults within your pack to play necessary and productive roles on your pack committee, including: secretary, advancement, public relations, religious emblems coordinator, event specific chairs, parent advocate, etc...

The opportunities to provide pack adults with a role to play in creating a stronger pack—your Scouts will love—in only an hour a week are nearly endless. As families volunteer, they will be more engaged, they will be more supportive and committed, and they may even have more fun. The adult that accepts a smaller role today may become a principle pack leader in the future. It is more the norm than the exception.

Chapter 3

Pack Program Planning

Studies demonstrate that strong, vibrant packs have an annual program plan that they prepare a year in advance. Most often, these are shared with pack families in the form of a calendar. Typically, annual program planning occurs during the summer.

There are several advantages of having an annual program plan for your pack.

- Your pack will attract more families to join when you can share specific program ideas you intend to deliver in the coming year
- Your pack will enjoy high retention rates for your Scouts
- You will have the foundations for creating a pack budget
- Your pack program plan and budget will make your popcorn program (or any other fund raising program) easier to communicate and deliver
- Your annual program plan will make it easier to deliver a steady and balanced flow of recognition for each den at each pack meeting
- You will have a clearer picture of volunteer assignments from higher commitment levels (den leader) to initial assignments (helping with the blue & gold celebration)

In short, if you desire a vibrant, growing pack with happy Scouts and adults who volunteer—you will want an annual program plan for your pack.

In preparation for creating your annual program plan, you will want gather calendar information:

1. Prior year program plans and budgets (if available) for reference
2. Family Talent Survey
    - If you have not already done so, conduct a Family Talent Survey of the adults associated with your pack. When you plan your program, this is an invaluable tool for identifying potential resources within your pack who may already have experience and interest in an area important to your plans.
    - You are far more likely to find adults who are receptive to volunteering when you are asking them to do something which they are familiar with and enjoy with some degree of expertise or comfort level

3. Scout Interest Survey
    - Consider capturing from the Scouts in each den their feedback on prior year(s) events and activities to explore what they might like to do again, what changes they might suggest, what new things they may have an interest in trying. It is not a bad idea to bring a list of new ideas under consideration to gain some feedback as well.

FAMILY TALENT SURVEY SHEET

**Each parent or adult family member should fill out a separate sheet
and turn it in at this meeting.**

Pack _____ Chartered Organization _____ Date _____

Welcome to the Cub Scout family of our pack. As explained to you, Cub Scouting is for parents as well as boys. We have a fine group of families who have indicated a willingness to help, according to their abilities. We invite you to add your talents and interests so that the best possible program can be developed for your boy and his friends.

Den leaders are always busy with den activities. Our pack leaders and committee members know you have some talent that will help in the operation of our pack. Although your help may not be on a full-time basis, whatever you can do will be appreciated.

In making this survey, your pack committee wants to uncover ways you can enjoy giving assistance. Please answer the following as completely as possible:

1. My hobbies are: _____

2. I can play and/or teach these sports: _____

3. My job, business, or profession would be of interest to Cub Scouts: _____

4. I am willing to help my boy and the pack as: ☐ pack committee member, ☐ Cub Scout den leader or assistant, ☐ Tiger Cub den leader, ☐ assistant Cubmaster, ☐ Webelos den leader or assistant, ☐ Cubmaster, ☐ Pack trainer.

5. My Scouting experience: Cub Scout _____ Boy Scout _____ Girl Scout _____

   Explorer _____ Rank attained _____

   Adult leader _____

6. I can help in these areas:

General Activities

☐ Carpentry ☐ Computer Skills
☐ Swimming ☐ Drawing/art
☐ Games ☐ Radio/electricity
☐ Nature ☐ Dramatics/skits
☐ Sports ☐ Cooking/banquets
☐ Outdoor activities ☐ Sewing
☐ Crafts ☐ Transportation
☐ Music/songs ☐ Other _____
☐ Bookkeeping _____

Special Program Assistance

☐ I have an SUV or ☐ van or ☐ truck.
☐ I have a workshop.
☐ I have family camping gear.
☐ I can make contacts for special trips and activities.
☐ I have access to a cottage or camping property
   or a boat.
☐ I can help Webelos Scouts with Boy Scout skills.
☐ I can, or know others who can, help with our Cub
   Scout Academics and Sports program.
☐ I can give other help. _____

Webelos Activity Areas

☐ Aquanaut ☐ Family Member ☐ Readyman
☐ Artist ☐ Fitness ☐ Scholar
☐ Athlete ☐ Forester ☐ Scientist
☐ Citizen ☐ Geologist ☐ Showman
☐ Communicator ☐ Handyman ☐ Sportsman
☐ Craftsman ☐ Naturalist ☐ Traveler
☐ Engineer ☐ Outdoorsman

Name _____ Home phone _____
Street address _____ Business phone _____
E-mail address _____ City _____ State _____ ZIP _____
Your cooperation and help are appreciated.

Example of a Family Talent Survey

See your district executive or unit commissioner for a copy

4. Key Dates
    - Dates and events of importance to your chartered organization
    - Important school & community dates and events
    - District and council dates that may affect your pack or leaders
    - Any other important dates that may affect the availability of your pack leaders or youth members

5. Pack Program Guides and Resources
    - Den meeting plans
    - Pack meeting plans
    - Other materials or guides containing program ideas for your den or pack activities. You will want to be able to refer to the "Guide to Safe Scouting" or "Age Appropriate Guidelines for Scouting Activities" documents. There are multiple other guides and resources available at www.Scouting.org, as well as on E-Bay, Scouter blogs, etc... (I share some of the more helpful sites that I have used in a later chapter) Consult with your unit commissioner or roundtable staff if you need more help in finding these.

An annual program planning meeting is an excellent opportunity to build excitement and unity within your pack leaders and families. While is can be a challenge to find a mutually agreeable date—the more folks who play a role in building your program plan, the more buy-in you will have when delivering it to your Scouts.

Consider inviting the following people to participate in your annual program plan meeting:

- Pack committee members
- Institutional head and chartered organization representative
- Den leaders
- Den chiefs
- District executive
- Unit commissioner
- Pack family adults

In my opinion, many organizations, Scouting included, can fall into a trap at this point of the planning process. There is often great momentum to begin filling in events and activities—after all, seeing the calendar fill in has the appearance of progress. I recommend a little more patience by investing in a brief discussion first, to obtain some agreement on what is most important to your pack—as a means for prioritizing program ideas to follow.

For example—in our pack, we agreed upon the following objectives:

1. We would plan so that Scouts could earn their rank badge in time for a February blue & gold celebration
2. We wished to establish a "brand" for our unit to include: advancement, service, conservation, personal achievement and outdoor activities
   - Our program would include elements that allowed Scouts to earn multiple Arrow Points, having achieved their badge of rank
   - We would have fall and spring camping events for all Scouts towards earning the outdoor activity award
   - Our program year would include several service projects so our Scouts could earn or repeat qualifying for the Good Turn for America award
   - Our program would include elements allowing our Scouts to earn or re-qualify for the Leave No Trace award
   - Our program would promote and encourage Scouts to explore personal interests and recognition through individualized pursuit of religious emblems and Cub Scouts Academic and Sports program (belt loops)
   - Encourage all Webelos Scouts to earn the Arrow of Light and transition to Boy Scouts

3. We would focus on one solid fund raising effort for the year and by selling popcorn—do our fair share to support the district and council (in addition to FOS donations)
4. No actively involved Scout would be turned away based on a lack of funds

5. Based on our area being less affluent—our uniform would focus on the field uniform shirt, neckerchief and insignia (with pants and other accessories being optional)

6. In order to assist den leaders, Scout advancement and community visibility of Scouting—the pack provided Scout manuals, rank associated neckerchiefs and pack activity T-shirts as a part of our program

7. We wished to qualify for summertime pack and quality unit status

8. Our pack and den meeting dates would avoid roundtable dates so our leaders could obtain the benefits of these events for the advantage of our Scouts

(Roundtables are monthly training sessions for adult leaders where best practices are shared. Your unit commissioner can get you further information)

9. Our pack would be visible, enthusiastic and productive participants in local school and community events so that we would avoid only being seen when we conduct our own recruiting events

Your list does not have to be very long—but you will find it helps when selecting and prioritizing events and activities or when placing them onto your pack events calendar.

The next step in the process is to brainstorm to gather ideas for activities and events your pack may wish to include in your program plan. It can be surprising how one idea can generate others—so for now, let ideas flow as freely as possible—there will be time to assess, tweak or prioritize later in the process.

Now you can begin assembling your program plan. It may be helpful to begin by noting the key dates collected earlier. They would include dates to avoid, as well as events you wish the pack or dens to play a part in.

Using the pack objectives you previously identified, review your brainstorming ideas and prioritize them based on how well they help you realize your objectives as well as fit within your remaining available dates.

You should now have a rough cut plan by den and pack with dates and topics. It may be helpful to construct this list as both a calendar view as well as a list. For your list view, it is a good idea to add the person responsible for each event. This will also help identify gaps—where you may need more volunteers to lend a hand.

Any event will likely have further sub-plans; however, there is time to add this detail later (unless the event occurs in the next month or two) so that you don't make this annual program planning meeting too long or too detailed. As long as you have a lead person identified—there is someone who will have the assignment to pull people together in the future to make sure all the necessary details are spelled out, assigned and communicated to make the event a success.

Based on prior annual program plans and budgets—create a rough cut budget based on this current plan. These may still be rough figures at this point—but you will want them to be at least directionally correct. Ultimately, you will want some visibility of the budget per rank, budget per Scout and budget per month (in relation to cash flow and pack cash reserves). Re-balance as necessary.

As you are completing your annual program plan—take a moment to assess it based on four views:

1. Does it align with your pack objectives?
2. Does it provide that potential to recognize every Scout for either den or pack advancement or achievement at every pack meeting?
3. Can the budget required to deliver it be sustained by the families in your pack?
4. Does the recognition schedule and budget for this plan appear to be equitably balanced across each rank?

Make any final adjustments based on the evaluation of the four views above and you now have an annual program plan that you can share with all the families of your pack.

You will want to consider how you will share this information with your pack families as well as how to keep it current.

Consider holding a special meeting with pack families to hand out and review the annual program plan. This is a perfect opportunity to whip up excitement for the coming pack year. It may also be the best time to begin cultivating volunteers to assist with upcoming events. I believe it is also the most opportune time to promote your fund raising plan as a means of making your program plan affordable for your pack families. Discuss with your pack families how you intend to communicate date or program changes that may be necessary to share in the future. This will help avoid confusion or miscommunication later.

You can now use this annual program plan at future pack committee meetings to make sure the necessary progress is being made to complete the more detailed plans—or if further assistance is needed to allow things to go more smoothly for your Scouts and families.

Congratulations! You now have an annual program plan. This is quite an accomplishment and one that is proven to be a key contributor to vibrant, healthy units. With this foundation built, you are well on your way towards building a stronger pack—your Scouts will love—in only an hour a week.

Not an official BSA publication and the BSA is not responsible for its content

Our Scout's uniforms also represented the brand for our pack (see photo above)

- Badges of rank were <u>earned</u> each year
- Arrow Points were earned via den plans as well as through the personal interests and initiative of individual Scouts

- Religious Emblems and Cub Scouts Academics and Sports program (belt loops) express the individual Scout's interests and initiative
  - Recruiter strips (with Cub Scout devices used to represent multiples) show how we so quickly grew our pack. Most of our Scouts earned these since they naturally wanted their friends to join in the fun.
  - Outdoor activity award on pocket flap showed we were active outside. In addition to other outings, we used the Cub Adventure Camp venues at Camp Cutler, located in Naples, N.Y. each spring and fall. Many of our Scouts also attended the summer program at this Seneca Waterways Council Reservation.
  - Good Turn for America patch demonstrated service to others
  - Leave No Trace patch demonstrated responsibility for the environment and an interest in ecology
  - Quality Unit patches were displayed on the right sleeve
  - One of our activities was helping Scouts make their own neckerchief slide. These were easy and inexpensive to make, did not slide off during activities (how many metal neckerchief slides have you found or replaced?) and did not need to be replaced each year with rank advancement.
  - Over 85% of our Scouts earned these badges through the design of our annual program plan. As you can see, this makes for happy Scouts.

What is your pack's brand?

Chapter 4

Budgets and Fund Raising

Now that an annual program plan has been created, our next step is creating a budget capable of funding the delivery of this program. By creating a sound budget and fund raising plan that meets your intended program needs, you will be well on your way to building a stronger pack—your Scouts will love—in only an hour a week.

Our first step is to forecast the annual expenses for the pack:

- **Registration, insurance, etc...**
- **Boys' Life fees**
  What boy would not value receiving a magazine in the mailbox each month filled with content that has been proven to be of interest to boys of their age? I strongly recommend investing in this valuable tool for your Scouts. So much so—in families where there is more than one boy in Scouting, I recommend they each receive their own copy. Keep the boy's perspective in mind when considering this.

- **Advancement and recognition requirements**
  Based on your intended program delivery (badges, pins, belt loops, cards, certificates, etc...). Consider into this estimate any recognition also intended for family members or adult leaders.

- **Program costs**

  The pack and den plans do a nice job of identifying materials and supplies required to achieve the objectives of these meetings. You will also want to budget for other program costs like pinewood derby expenses, blue & gold celebration expenses and expected field trips and outings (including campouts). Our twice per year pack campouts were always held at council sponsored campsites. Not only did this support the investment of our council in providing high quality facilities, but it gave our Scouts and their families a broader view of Scouting by seeing so many Scouts from other units there. We also felt that Scout handbooks, neckerchiefs and activity T-shirts were important to our program and included these in our budgeting as well.

Your pack committee may need to consider a policy regarding program expenses. In our pack, all Scouting related expenses for the Scout were covered in the dues—with any incremental family expenses (like food for family members accompanying us on campouts) being a la cart. This helped to account for varying family sizes and levels of participation.

Training

Your pack committee may also need to establish a policy regarding training fees for leaders. There appears to be no standard for this. In our pack, leaders paid for their own training, but the pack paid for leader earned insignia—which we incorporated as a part of our recognition program in pack meetings for the benefit of our leaders, Scouts and their families.

Other expenses

Your pack may wish to include other factors in your budget. Some packs seek to maintain a reserve fund that can be used to defray initial expenses to register new Scouts until dues are collected. These funds can also be tapped for camperships or other pack committee supported uses.

Our second step is to identify all sources of income anticipated for the coming year. This includes dues expected from existing and expected new Scouts. If your pack is chartered by an organization that financially supports your unit, this funding will also offset planned expenses. The balance, if any, will need to be covered through direct payments from Scout families or through fund raising activities.

Typically, you will want to establish a goal per Scout. Please note, aside from formally structured fund raising programs like Scouting Popcorn, fund raising efforts must be reviewed and approved in advance by your district executive, via the "Unit Money-Earning Permit" application. Your unit commissioner can help you get this process started. More on fund raising later...

Having established program, budget and fund raising goals, you are now ready to communicate your total plan with your pack families.

Scouting Popcorn

I would like to share some perspectives regarding popcorn sales. Keep in mind; I have now experienced this fund raising phenomenon as a Cubmaster, a district commissioner, a district chair, a council board member, and as a parent.

When my son and I first joined Cub Scouts, our pack was decidedly against popcorn sales. Apparently, the pack did sell popcorn in the past, but the experience influenced families to pursue other options—hence our 3 (or more) fund raisers in that year. We ran fund raisers ranging from first aid kits, to candy bars, to flowers in order to avoid selling popcorn. These efforts did generate funds for the pack, enabling us to deliver our intended program.

As I became more involved in the pack as a leader, I learned more about the popcorn program. While I wasn't opposed to the fund raisers we had used, I didn't care for the need to run a multiple of programs throughout our Scouting year. It seemed we might be more focused on raising money than delivering program. I came to learn a few things about the popcorn program that changed my perspective:

- Selling popcorn <u>is</u> a part of our program for Scouts.
  - o Selling popcorn introduces Scouts to several important life experiences (planning & goal setting, selling, public speaking, money management)
  - o Selling popcorn provides our Scouts very tangible recognition and rewards for their efforts. (dues, prizes, the pride of having provided at least some of the means for paying for their Scouting experience)

- 70% of popcorn sales return back to Scouting (council, district, pack, Scouts).
- Council has payment terms with the vendor that allow units to run sales over an extended period prior to payment. With some other fundraisers, we only had 2 weeks to sell before the invoice for the products was due. Given our pack treasury balance (or lack thereof)—this limited our options as a pack and put unnecessary selling pressure on our families.
- While a $1 candy bar may make for a quick sale, you need to sell a lot of them to match the power of selling popcorn.
- With some planning, you may only need <u>one</u> solid fund raising effort each year to fund your Scouting program. If this is not the case for your unit, speak to your unit commissioner so they can arrange to get you some help from your district committee for next year's fund raiser.
- I have found that many people really love our popcorn products for their flavor, variety and quality. Others truly enjoy the opportunity to purchase products from our Scouts as an expression of their support for Scouting. Some buy for both reasons.
- Selling can be a means for recruiting for your unit. We meet many families while doing take-orders and show and sells and this gives us an opportunity to talk about Scouting and invite the families we meet to come and check out a Scout meeting.

- Some of our families came to learn that selling popcorn could be an economic equalizer for the pack. Our families came from a range of socio-economic circumstances. For families with lower discretionary cash reserves, selling popcorn could fund <u>all</u> of their incremental expenses for Scouting. Ask you district executive or unit commissioner how this could be achieved for your families.

Our pack made the decision to return to using the popcorn program. We attended the training provided by the council, integrated it into our annual program plan and found that we could fund our needs through one fund raising effort a year. Our third year into popcorn, we found that achieving our sales goals became a little simpler each year as we gained experience. We do still get the occasional pack family that finds selling popcorn to be a challenge. To help, we set up one or two Show and Sell opportunities each year to help those families that just can't seem to sell enough to meet their needs through their own neighborhood or family connections.

If your pack does not presently fund raise using the popcorn program, I hope these few passages might influence you to reconsider. If you are a Scout family that finds this time of the year a challenge, perhaps some of these perspectives will help you to better embrace the experience. There is a saying, "if the prize is big enough, the work doesn't matter." If the prize was merely the money we earn from selling popcorn, make no mistake, there is effort in it. However, if you can step back and see your Scout don his uniform with pride and stretch and grow to go out there and meet customers, make the sale and collect the proceeds so he can play a role in paying his own way (and maybe earn a sales incentive prize), then perhaps you will find a new perspective in the experience.

I would also offer pack leadership this advice... If you find your pack families are resistant to selling popcorn to raise funds, consider your approach for introducing the topic.

We found that when we gathered our Scouts and families to share our annual program plan for the coming year, they became very excited about all the fun and interesting events and activities that we had planned to do together. We also made sure to mention the recognition that would be earned throughout the year as we progressed through our plan. Having completed this (including as much eye-candy as possible with props like soda-bottle rocket launchers, pinewood derby cars and soon-to-be earned patches) it was a smooth transition into how to pay for the cost of delivering such a program.

Folks could see that we had budgeted responsibly and also had balanced the expense, as well as the achievements, very evenly across all dens and ranks. We then introduced popcorn as a way to offset the cost—for some families, it became a means of offsetting the cost totally—should they decide to sell enough popcorn.

Now that folks could see the value in the annual program, and that popcorn was a means for paying for it—we rolled out a simple plan that would help all families reach this goal with Show and Sells and Take-Orders. We shared how we would teach Scouts how to sell as a part of our den meetings and that we had leaders standing by to make things go as simply as possible.

It is no accident that Scouting has created program aids offering instant recognition as Scouts progress towards earning their badge of rank. Imagine if there was no recognition from September until a February blue and gold celebration? So if the recognition beads provided for Tiger Cubs and Cub Scouts and the Webelos pins provided for Webelos Scouts make sense for advancement—why wouldn't you wish to have some type of progressive recognition for your fund raising efforts?

It may be your council popcorn program already has some selling incentives in place. I would encourage your pack to consider setting your own incentives (either to supplement the council goal or to replace it). In some instances, the council goals for incentive prizes may be set higher than what is needed for your pack to fund your annual program needs. We found that if the selling goal was too large—too few families found it to be any incentive at all. We established a prize incentive consistent with our pack goals. We found it provided a meaningful incentive so that the Scouts achieved their fund raising goal in nearly 100% of the families. Those were mighty proud Scouts when at the pack meeting—they were asked to come forward to accept the praise of the pack and their incentive prize. We simply embedded the cost of the prizes into our overall pack goal.

I learned as a Cubmaster that a portion of the popcorn sales profits go to fund the council and district. It had not occurred to me as a Tiger Cub parent that my son's registration fee went to national and our dues went to the pack annual program plan. As I received invaluable council provided support through roundtables and training classes—I came to value the timeliness of these resources. We were also blessed with the availability of a tremendous Cub Scout Adventure Camp owned by our council. Our Scouts and families shared many special moments camping at these facilities twice a year (not to mention their incredible summertime program). Your council and district depend upon a portion of the popcorn sale profits to fund their contribution to Scouting too.

When our pack decided to forego popcorn sales in favor of first aid kits, candy bars and flower, we were only raising funds for our own pack purposes. We were not providing our fair share towards council and district resources that we were clearly benefiting from. I am proud that our decision to return to popcorn sales rectified this oversight. It feels more consistent with the Scout Oath and Laws we teach our Scouts.

The Ships—located at Camp Cutler, in Naples, New York

Chapter 5

Recruiting Scouts

Having established an annual program plan (what you are going to do) and a budgeting and fund raising plan (how it will be paid for), you now can answer some key questions that you might be asked if a family wants to join your pack. Let's now explore how to go and find them.

Many packs are experiencing a decline in unit membership. There can be many possible root causes for this trend. Some areas simply have fewer Scout age boys than in prior years. For the boys in an area who might join Scouting, there are now numerous other activities they might also enjoy—many of which will require much higher degrees of time commitment than Scouting, seemingly crowding the opportunity to join a pack out of the picture. There are countless other causes for the trend—but I may be the only person in Scouting to tell you that all of these trends and reasons don't really matter to you or your pack or den.

The truth is, as long as we focus on national or community generalities, these issues mentioned will appear to be an obstacle to Scouting. But when we get right down to the fact of the matter—as far as your son is concerned, Scouting is all about your pack. In my opinion, well intended efforts to turnaround the membership trend in Scouting cannot succeed if only approached at the national, council or even district level. No matter how hard they try, how much money they invest or how noble their efforts—they simply lack the one secret ingredient to exploding pack membership—you.

If your pack is serious about recruiting more Scouts (and with them, more volunteers) you will need to do two things.

The first thing we have covered. Prepare an exciting annual program plan that will result in your Scouts having fun and earning recognition that they can celebrate with their families. Strong program sells and the excitement it generates retains the Scouts you have and attracts the friends they know.

The second thing is to leverage the power of the word-of-mouth credibility you and your Scouts have with the people you know and see every day, who are not already a part of the Scouting program.

You, and your Scout, are the most effective secret weapon Scouting has to attract more Scouts. Nothing else can touch this. Your positive encouragement to other adults you know to stop by your pack or den event and simply check things out cannot be matched by the most well designed flyer, radio spot, newspaper article or TV ad.

If your recruiting efforts are to be successful, it is critical your Scouts and their family members actively encourage their friends and neighbors to check out Scouting and tell them how much they enjoy being a part of your pack. The power is yours to share.

Every pack has one or two charismatic adults that people just naturally listen to and follow. They are not always the official leader in the group—but if you are observant, you can always tell who they are. For whatever reason, their opinion has the power to influence others and people pay attention to them. If you can get them to engage as an influencer for your recruiting efforts, to serve as a parent advocate, you will suddenly find an explosion of interest from the church committee or PTO or other parent related organizations that exist around your pack. Keep in mind that in order to perform this role, you are merely asking this person to do what they already do naturally. They do not need to put on a uniform or take a lot of training or commit a lot of time. Simply tell all the people you know why Scouting is important to you and your family and why you feel it would be important to others as well. You just can't match this kind of energy and impact with e-mail blasts and flyers.

Shortly, I will share how we taught our Scouts how to invite a friend to our events. These skills on how to invite, how to follow-up and how to follow-through are important life skills. We may as well get double duty out of the lesson by making the pack stronger while we practice these skills. After-all, our Scouts will be rewarded twice… They will earn a recruiter strip badge for their uniform and they will now be able to share the fun they have in Scouting with a personal friend.

In my Scouting area, we have enjoyed solid success utilizing a joining event model that is highly dependent upon access to schools. Where access to schools is available, this model remains effective. A somewhat recent challenge has been a disruption in this model due to less Scouting access to youth through schools. Theories abound as to why there may be less access—or why there is more competition today than ever before for a Scouting family's time, etc… Rather than get distracted by these issues, I'm going to stay focused on some proven approaches to Cub Scout recruitment so that, in spite of all the challenges folks can identify, you can grow your membership by building a stronger pack—your Scouts will love—in only an hour a week.

Before we get into the nuts and bolts of recruiting, it may be important for your pack to reconsider your collective view of recruiting new Scouts. Some packs only recruit in the fall. Some packs recruit in the fall and spring. Some packs recruit year-round. I would urge your pack to adopt the practice of actively recruiting year-round. It is always a good day to invite a new Scout and their family into the world of Scouting.

I would also strongly encourage you to consider how your pack's visibility is seen by the local community. If the only time your community knows you are there is during your recruiting period—you may be short changing your program. If your pack is seen as a positive and active part of a wide-range of community events—you will find local families will want to be a part of such a positive influence in their community whose members "walk the walk" and not just show up on their own recruiting day. Make sure your annual program plan includes key school and community events where your pack can demonstrate that it is a productive and happy contributor to important highlights within the community. Whether by wearing your field uniforms or your activity t-shirts, your pack presence at these events will make a favorable impact. After all, even the casual observer will notice Scouting in action.

One of the challenges of year-round recruiting is when a new Scout joins a den that has already progressed through some of their requirements for the program year. This can potentially create an issue for the new Scout family, as well as the den leader. As early as possible, try to establish a clear understanding of expectations regarding helping a new Scout to catch up with the den, between the den leader and the Scout's family. Most families are fine starting from the moment where they joined the den within the program year. Others are motivated to catch their Scouts up to speed with prior completed requirements. With the Scout family adults serving as Akela—catching up (on all or even some requirements and achievement) can often be accomplished by having them follow the den meeting planner notes used for prior meetings. Each family can assess their own capability and desire to do this.

An additional benefit of this approach is that any Scout family that demonstrates the capability and commitment to catch their Scout up to speed with their den by using the den meeting planner notes are prime candidates for volunteer roles within your pack. Using this approach means that catching up a new Scout with the rest of the den does not need to be an additional responsibility expected of your den leaders. Letting your den leaders know this will go a long ways towards adopting a year-round recruiting mindset for your pack.

Let's cover the traditional joining event model. This model assumes your pack can arrange with the local school to conduct a School Night for Scouting—along with the ability to promote the event ahead of time through take-home flyers and boy talks. Boy talks are a brief presentation made to

Cub Scout age boys by a district executive or volunteer during the school day. Many times, it is scheduled for the day of the School Night for Scouting event. Flyers typically contain key information for attending the School Night for Scouting event and are either distributed physically as a take-home document for parent's attention or distributed electronically by the school or parent-teacher organization.

At the School Night for Scouting event, information about the Cub Scout program, and the pack specifically, is shared with the attendees. Following a brief question and answer period, families fill out an application and are instructed when and where their next meeting with the pack or den will take place. When executed well—this process works like a charm.

Let's talk about some ideas that might make your joining event even more successful.

Timing

Timing matters. Our experience has been that the first couple of days of school in the fall are very hectic, both at school and at home. Who hasn't experienced their child falling asleep early during these first few days— exhausted by absorbing all the change? On the other hand—you don't want to be losing an entire month of den meetings. Similarly, in the spring, we tried to plan our joining events prior to the start of spring sports—where family evenings would be at a premium.

When considering a date for your joining event—I recommend selecting two different nights of the week, on successive weeks (two events total). This insulates your recruiting efforts from "that is a bad night for us" or "that was a bad week for us".

Promotion

Typically, in the School Night for Scouting model, schools will allow an information flyer to go home with students, in advance of your event. Many packs get tripped up by the logistics of preparing the flyer, getting it properly approved and getting the correct quantity to the right place at the right time so that they go home in time for a productive joining event. This is another reason to have a dedicated membership chair, so they can focus on getting these details right, without splitting their attention on preparing for the next den or pack meeting. Your district executive or unit commissioner can also be helpful in getting the details and logistics of producing and distributing joining event flyers correct.

In addition to flyers, schools will often allow for a "boy talk". In my area of Scouting, a boy talk is when a district executive or volunteer is allowed to meet with boys in the school on the day of a School Night for Scouting. Usually, in a brief chat, they can whip up a lot of enthusiasm on the part of the boys to attend the joining event with their families. The combination of the boy talk and the take-home flyers can generally create an impressive School Night for Scouting turn-out.

There are a couple of ways to make this turn-out even stronger. Our pack uses activity T-shirts (sometimes referred to as class-Bs in Scouting) for when an activity might be very messy and we would like to keep our field uniforms (also known as class-As) from taking a beating. Making pizzas at the local pizza shop comes to mind. We have found that our activity T-shirts can be worn at school the day of the boy talk or joining event. It allows the boys not presently in Scouting to see how many other boys are already involved in the pack. While the field uniform might make an even bigger impression, they are not always ideal for days when the Scouts have art or gym class. If your pack does not currently use activity T-shirts, this might be another reason to consider investing in them.

Another promotion tactic we used with great success in our pack was to incorporate into our den meetings some time to teach our Scouts how to invite a friend to attend a joining event—and how to follow through to confirm they would be coming. There are many ways to make this a fun lesson to learn—and it is an important life lesson to share.

I learned that it was relatively inexpensive to have simple business cards printed with my personal Scouting information on them (for example, Vista

Print will make 250 cards for $10). I had a few horizontal lines watermarked on the back side. We taught our Scouts to use the back side to write a simple invitation they could give to a friend that would tell them the date, time and place for our next joining event (or meeting). If the invited child's parent had a question, they could look on the flip side and contact me to get more information. You could also reference BeAScout.org or your pack's website (if you have one) for them to find more information as well. It is simple, works great and it is inexpensive.

Never underestimate the power of recognition. With this in mind, we always have a tenured Cub Scout model for others their recruiter strip—proudly sewn on their field uniform, under the right side shirt pocket. Don't just talk about it—let them see one on a Scout's uniform, or pass around one not yet sewn on. Let them know that if a boy they invite joins the pack, they can earn a Recruiter Strip for their field uniform, to be awarded to them at the next den and pack meeting. We even went a step further—for Scouts who had already earned a recruiter strip, we awarded them Cub Scout device pins to demonstrate they have successfully recruited a multiple of Scouts for the pack.

The Event

I have noticed that if the kids want to join, the parents want to join. Your primary audience, therefore, is the kids. Sure, adults will have questions, but most of these can be addressed in better detail at a later venue (like a den meeting) rather than during the joining event.

I believe we err towards convincing the adults to sign their kids up for Scouting. We over-focus on the adults, only to share so much information that the kids get bored, the adults get confused and in the process, we lose some Scouts. Keep in mind, if they took the time to come to your joining event—they are already pre-disposed to want to join. Make it simple for them to do so.

Our most productive joining events were those where our own Scouts entertained potential new Scouts through a variety of fun activities that represented the kinds of things Scouts do. Kids could freely rotate through various stations where they might try racing a pinewood derby car, or raingutter regatta boat or space derby rocket. They really seemed to like the small catapults that are available as crafts in the Scout Store. We would have them shoot wrapped hard candy through cut out targets. When we could recruit outside, we would have them launch soda bottle rockets or use a rope bridge. The important thing was they were doing Scouting things with our Scouts and having fun. Their families could see this.

One of our better ideas was to have them complete many of the requirements towards earning the Bobcat badge at each station they tried. Our final station was either a rope bridge (if outside) or a cross over bridge (if inside). As they crossed the bridge, we would give them a Bobcat card. We showed them what a Bobcat badge looked like and told them that if they showed up at our next den or pack meeting with that card—they could earn their first badge in Scouting! We recommended that the families go ahead and pick up a field uniform so they would have something to sew their new badges on.

The truth is the goal of your joining event is not simply to have them fill out an application. Your goal is to get them to come to the next planned meeting (den or pack) so that while the boy is actively participating in the meeting, pack leaders can quietly answer questions and assist family members in completing applications and making any initial payments. Believe me, when they go home with their Bobcat card—nothing will keep the boy and their family from showing up at the next meeting to get their badge. Of course, when they do so, they will complete the final two requirements (officially register as a Scout and complete the Scout handbook safety section with their adult). If you never see them again after the School Night for Scouting (doubtful) you are only out of the cost of the Bobcat card.

Some adults attending your joining event may wonder—but not ask—whether you really know how to deliver an effective program. They may be motivated by a desire to make sure their son is selecting a well running pack where they will have a lot of fun and benefit from advancement. They might also be trying to determine if the pack itself is running smoothly so they won't have to commit themselves to volunteer roles in order to make sure their son receives from the pack experience all the intentions shared at the joining event. The pro-active response to these natural questions is to show them that your pack:

- has a well-rounded program
- has a budget to deliver that program
- has the means to fund the budget
- has trained volunteers to deliver the program
- already has trained leaders recognized by Scouting for their personal effectiveness (leader knots)
- has a track record for youth advancement and recognition, including successfully transitioning Arrow of Light Scouts into the Boy Scout program
- has achieved bronze, silver or gold Journey to Excellence (or whatever is the current quality unit award program) demonstrating they are a top unit as benchmarked against other units nationally

If, at this point, your pack cannot demonstrate that all of these things are in place—this gives you some additional objectives to consider when putting together your annual program plan. If you have further questions about how to do or achieve some of these things—speak with your unit commissioner, they will be happy to help you.

If your pack can prepare a one or two page brochure about your pack to hand out at joining events—that should suffice towards providing attending adults some initial information about your pack leaders, contact information, pack program and what you plan to do for the coming year. This is another reason having your annual pack program figured out is so important to recruiting success. You will also know how your pack will handle dues and fees so that these questions can be summarized as well.

Let families know you can answer all of their specific questions during the next meeting, while their son is participating and then staff accordingly to do so—simultaneous, but separate from the den activities. This also gives you the advantage of providing more personalized attention since den sizes are only so big (ideally 6-8 Scouts) whereas a heavily attended joining event could have 12-30 (or more) families attending. How could you ever answer all the family specific questions in a single setting without boring the boys or needing a very long meeting?!

Sometimes, someone from the district is asked to collect the Scout applications from your joining event. To avoid disappointment, simply schedule them to attend your next den or pack meeting rather than your joining event—since that is the meeting where the applications and payments for registration will ultimately take place.

Lack of School Access Alternatives

As mentioned earlier, sometimes the traditional joining events and boy talk model cannot be used. Again, the key ingredient is to utilize the power of influence each of your Scouts and pack families have with friends, schoolmates, teammates and fellow worshippers by encouraging them personally to attend a joining event for your pack.

An alternative model that can be used when school access is a challenge is a community joining event. Pick a community location, like a park, and hold an open event broader than the local school. This event could be hosted by your district or council. Sometimes it is collaboration between a multiple of packs in the area. The approach is the same—offer fun activities that Scouts do and have your current Scouts invite their friends. Wherever a guest has been invited specifically by a member of a pack—make sure to steer them to an information booth where they can meet members of that pack. If anyone is attending due to a flyer (but not a specific pack invite) help them to find a pack that can meet their needs.

There are a couple of advantages of this community joining event model. Where school access is an issue, it allows us to still use much of the proven traditional joining event model. Also, where a given area may have lesser experienced pack leadership, this approach can help to teach them how to hold their own joining event in the future. Sometimes, a family's personal schedule just doesn't synch with the meeting schedule of a pack or den. At a community joining event, families are more likely to find some pack in their area where schedules can work.

When you think about it—when kids sign up for baseball or other sports, they are not always assigned to teams along with all of their friends. Some friends are assigned to the same team, whereas other friends get assigned to competing teams. This happens all the time and in spite of this, the kids and their families enjoy the sports season—and in the process make new friends from the teammates on their team that they did not know prior to the season.

Occasionally, in Scouting, folks get fixated upon all the kids they know joining the same pack. In instances where this works out, schedule-wise, that is fantastic. Keep this sports perspective in mind for those instances where, due to schedule issues, another pack might need to be considered. It would be a shame to miss the promise of Scouting due to an expectation that all the boys from the same class must be in the same pack. It is an expectation that is seldom fully met in other youth activities.

Today, there can be almost a year round expectation of focus and time commitment when involved in activities outside of Scouting. This can often feel like a pre-condition of earning a spot on next season's team. This pattern is not limited to sports. Compounding this pattern is the realization that only some of the boys will ever develop their skills to truly achieve the level of competence that brings regular playing time and achievement. Many of the others, in spite of many hours and dollars of commitment, will eventually succumb to natural selection—becoming the practice squad and injury replacement that allows the first team to practice for the next opponent.

I played many sports growing up and as an adult, and I coached youth baseball, softball and soccer. I am an enthusiastic advocate for youth sports. But the reality is that youth who play sports early in life experience a progressive weeding out process as skill levels mature.

My point is not to tear down sports—but to merely point out three aspects of Scouting that may offer adults who consider Scouting some relieve from this phenomenon.

1. When the sports season winds down, Scouting is here for your son for the balance of the year—to participate and advance at the pace you decide.

2. Every Scout plays—there is no second team or practice squad.

3. Although your son's den will be pursuing achievements consistent with their rank—Scouting also offers a tremendous range of topics your son can explore (either to demonstrate their prior earned expertise or to try things they had always been interested to do) that are unique to them. In all likelihood—while trying their best—they will come to learn that they will earn some mighty nice recognition for doing so. You can't always experience this in sports.

A couple of final points... spring recruiting is a powerful accelerator for your pack membership. A Tiger Cub den started in the spring and nurtured through the summer by your summertime pack program will get your fall recruiting off to an incredible start. After all, you will already have Tiger Cub Scouts and parents to help you recruit—and likely a Tiger Cub den leader as well.

One way to reach incoming Tiger Cubs is to explore with your existing pack families, any connections they may have with families with kindergarten age kids. Someone always knows an influential parent whose opinion other parents listen to. Connecting early with these influential parents can often bring a huge turnout to your joining event. Just like kids like to join other kids, parents will appreciate joining a group with positive energy and positive association.

In addition to starting up new Tiger Cub dens, every time our pack recruited in the spring we picked up a few Scouts at every rank. You will also appreciate that more Scouts also means more volunteers.

I have witnessed joining events across many packs. I am convinced the difference between a pack experiencing a tremendous response of new Scouts or a trickle is the active support it receives from its leaders and packs families. My observations tell me that when a joining event is held by only a leader or two—turnout will generally be light.

When a majority of the packs leaders, Scouts and families attend the joining event, there is almost always a huge turnout of new Scouts who wish to join. Which result do you want? Do your pack a big favor. When planning a joining event, take the time to call your Scouts and pack families and personally encourage them to attend and to bring their non-Scouting friends to join the fun. More friends mean more fun, and more fun mean more friends. This is how Scouting grows.

Recruiting success is a key element towards building a stronger pack— your Scouts will love—in only an hour a week. If you would like more information, see your unit commissioner—they are there to serve and can connect you with resources developed to help you by your district and council membership committee.

The Pioneer Fort—located at Camp Cutler, in Naples, New York

Chapter 6

Developing Volunteers

As we discussed in the chapter on pack structure, one of the keys to building a stronger pack—your Scouts will love—in only an hour a week is to share the work of running the pack across a broader number of volunteers. Let's talk about how to do that...

One of the amazing things about Scouting is that it is really operated and sustained by volunteers. Given how many of us feel our lives are getting busier year by year—the fact that Scouting can attract so many high caliber volunteers is a testimony to the passion adults feel about making a difference for the youth in their communities.

Considering that even if a brand new volunteer to Scouting was a Scout in their youth—the role to be played by a Scouting volunteer is a new experience for all of us. To make a volunteer driven organization effective— we need to provide some training so people will know what to do as well as how to do it.

Finally, given the potential for polarizing viewpoints on politics, religion, sports teams, schools, etc... it is amazing to me how well a collection of volunteers can set aside what may divide us in order to focus on a common cause that unites us. This is Scouting...

Recall that in Tiger Cubs, we ask each family to play a role throughout the year in helping the Tiger Cub den leader to run the meeting and deliver program. If your pack is experiencing difficulties in getting adults to step forward to volunteer to help, it may be because you have not leveraged this aspect of the Tiger Cub den as effectively as possible. Let's explore this deeper.

Approximately 15% of adults are natural born leaders. These are the folks who will naturally fill a void in leadership and are the most likely to step forward to lead when another leader is not already present. As it turns out, we like to approach den sizes of about 6-8 Scouts. There are many underlying reasons for this being the ideal size for a den.

- It is the same number boys will eventually experience in patrols
- There are enough boys that they can play games and have fun— while not being lost in a larger group
- The den is not so large as to prohibit meeting in a den member's home versus requiring a much larger venue, ...

Another plus (while it does not always automatically work out this way) is that this means for every 6-8 Tiger Cubs there will be at least one natural born volunteer who will agree to become the Tiger Cub den leader. Occasionally, during the initial gathering of a new Tiger Cub den, you will find the attending Tiger Cub parents to be a bit tentative about jumping forward to claim the Tiger Cub den leader role. This is not unusual, and you should anticipate this possibility. It is important to be firm about the Scouting model that it is the adults of the den that volunteer, working together to deliver the program to the Scouts. Keep in mind also the saying "if you need something done, give it to a busy person". If you do not jump in too quickly to agree with the den adults on how busy they all are—you will almost always ultimately find your den leader.

In cases where you find a particularly reluctant group of adults—take some encouragement that, in spite of their expressed busy lifestyles, they have all decided to make some time in order to bring their sons to the den meeting.

So, the issue is a lot less about time and a lot more about comfort zone and trust. They are not yet comfortable with or feel they fully understand the added scope of the den leader role and/or they are not yet sure they can trust your assistance should they find that they need help.

Jumping back to our pack structure chapter—a powerful role for an experienced pack volunteer is pack trainer. Often, the volunteers who fill this position are former den leaders or Cubmasters. Your council offers very effective training for pack trainers to help them better understand the role and deliver its benefits to your pack. If you have a pack trainer, the approach I am about to share would be a perfect role for them to fill. If your pack does not yet have a pack trainer, your Cubmaster may be the person to fill this role.

Gather your Tiger Cub den parents, apart from the Scouts, and share with them copies of the Tiger Cub den meeting planners. These are 1-2 page scripts describing every aspect of how to prepare, run and wrap-up a specific den meeting. (They are available for all ranks, as well as for pack meetings). Recall that these can be easily purchased at your local Scout store, or downloaded for free at Scouting.org. Your unit commissioner can help you find them.

Depending on how detailed your annual pack program planning process is, you might have already selected the meeting plans and sequence for your den year. One really good reason to select these plans and their sequence during annual program planning is that you can confirm through these plans that you will have monthly advancement and recognition by the den, which will give all of your Scouts and their family's motivation to actively attend all of your pack meetings.

A second motivation for using these den meeting plans is they simplify the process of creating a reliable pack budget. When you are recruiting volunteers to serve as den leaders, these den meeting plans are a simple way to demonstrate that as a den leader, they will be able to deliver strong program to the den—the Scouts will love—in only an hour a week. One of your objections from a potential volunteer has been addressed.

This exercise also allows you to address the second objection (will you be there for me if I get into trouble) because you have "walked the walk" by sitting down with the den adults to demonstrate the materials available to them to make the den leader role easier. You can further reinforce this message a couple of ways.

I mentioned earlier in the book, a national study that was conducted to explore what makes a successful pack. One of the key elements was training. During this session, let your den adults know about training that Scouting offers to help them better understand their role and how to do it. We offer both in-class and on-line options to facilitate busy schedules. Make sure you also mention your district offers the opportunity to share learning and fellowship on a monthly basis through your roundtable meetings (better yet, offer to take them to the next one). Finally, by the very fact that you have personally taken the time to sit with the group to help them get off to a great start—you have demonstrated that you will make yourself available as an experienced resource once they get underway.

In our pack, we took this session one step further. We had our Tiger Cub den families rotate through a schedule where they helped the Tiger Cub den leader run the meeting. Given this practice, it made every sense to share with them the Tiger Cub den meeting plans, so they would better understand the intended content (and their role) for the meeting they were assisting. This practice had several positive effects:

- The Tiger Cub den leader automatically received incremental help for running the meeting. Sometimes, just knowing you are sharing the load helps lessen some of the concern.
- Tiger Cub den families were automatically more invested in the success of the den and the pack.
- Having helped "co-lead", den families were often more supportive and less critical of the formal den leader. After all, it always looks easier to do from the passive back of the room
- Perhaps most importantly, we were teaching Tiger Cub den adults how to volunteer. We would have four more years to leverage that positive experience.

By the way, we used the very same technique in our Wolf Scout, Bear Scout and Webelos Scout dens to engage our families in the active delivery of our den meeting plans. Why stop at Tiger Cubs if it is working and you find your families enjoy helping?

A hard won truth is that you likely need to train your pack families on how to volunteer. Once you have a Tiger Cub den leader (leveraging the statistical probability that in a group of 6-8 families you will find at least one natural leader), you can now pursue the process of teaching your other adults how they can help the pack, on their own terms. The better you are at doing this, the better your success will be at building a stronger pack—your Scouts will love—in only an hour a week.

A terrific tool for packs is the Family Talent Survey (an example can be found earlier in this book). Through the use of this tool, you can learn about the interests and the expertise of the families within your pack. This can help you select program ideas that you can be more certain your pack families will love. It also helps you identify areas where your pack adults (volunteers) already have a passion for and comfort zone to discuss or talk about.

There are many roles that adults can fill beyond the den leader and Cubmaster openings. Frequently, the best way to develop your next den leader or Cubmaster is to get them to progressively fill a need they are comfortable doing now. Look for these opportunities as often as possible. The Webelos Scout den leader of tomorrow may be the same person that a few years earlier was talked into taking candid photos of a pack meeting or pinewood derby race. This is in fact, more the norm.

Keep in mind also that while an adult may not be comfortable, at first, with the full responsibility of a larger pack event—like your blue and gold celebration—they may be very happy to serve on your blue and gold celebration committee with responsibility for decorations, etc... You never know, from such humble beginnings may rise your next committee chair.

Studies have shown that one of the biggest obstacles to getting pack adults to volunteer is that they did not know there was a need to be filled. While the need for a den leader may be more obvious—there are many roles to be filled (some year round, some part time) if you wish to build a stronger pack—your Scouts will love—in only an hour per week. Given the study results, a positive first step you can take to finding volunteers is to have a list that describes the roles you would like someone to fill. Honestly, sometimes it is really that simple. One of the powerful benefits of having an annual pack program plan is that you will be able to identify both larger and smaller sized roles for volunteers to fill. This provides that added advantage of seeing how you might get someone started on a smaller role today—in preparation for accepting a larger role tomorrow that they might not necessarily be comfortable accepting straight on.

Another lesson I have learned is that you cannot simply place a clipboard of the open roles on a table or send it out in an e-mail and expect many people to read it and then contact you to fill the role. Too bad, that approach seemed so efficient...

The good news is, I have learned that more often than not—if you ask someone to fill a specific role, and you can define for them what that is, they will agree to give it a try. You dramatically upgrade your chances of success if you initially ask them to do something they are either passionate about—or already have a comfort doing. This is why the Family Talent Survey can be a terrific tool for creating a plan for developing pack volunteers.

You may find that at certain times, it is how you ask for volunteers that can make all the difference. I have learned of and used some very effective approaches for getting potential volunteers to consider stepping forward to fill a role in Scouting. I will share a summary of them here—but you can learn more about them by asking your unit commissioner.

The following is a great story, but for the greatest impact and effectiveness—don't just tell this story—physically act it out. In fact, this is a terrific skit to perform in front of both your Scouts and your families. It is an important message for them all. I have used it as a Cubmaster minute in pack meetings with great reception. I can also tell you that if you perform the skit by substituting the rocks, pebbles and sand with different size candy—the kids love it.

A committee chair picked up a large empty jar and proceeded to fill it with small rocks. She asked the pack, "Is the jar full?"

They unanimously agreed that the jar was full.

So, the committee chair picked up a box of pebbles and poured them into the jar. She shook the jar lightly and the pebbles rolled into the open areas between the rocks.

She then asked the pack "Now is the jar full?

Again, they unanimously agreed that the jar was full.

Then the committee chair picked some sand and poured it into the jar. Of course, the sand filled in the open cracks and crevices even further.

"Now," the committee chair said, "I want you to see how this jar of rocks is like your life. The rocks are the important things: your family, your partner, your friends, your health, your children, and things that if everything else was lost and only they remained, your life would still be full.

The pebbles are the other things that matter like your job, your house, your car. The sand is all the other lesser important stuff."

"It is interesting to note that each time I asked you if the jar was full—it seemed as though it was. Yet we were able to find ways to continue to fit more things in—if we were willing to shake things around a little bit."

"It is equally, if not more important, to note that if you put the sand into the jar first, there is no room for the pebbles or the rocks. The same goes for your life. If you spend all your time and energy on the small stuff, you will never have room for the things that are important to you."

"Our pack is run by volunteers—each of whom likely entered into Scouting with a jar that already seemed full. Each of our current volunteers had to reconsider what were the larger rocks versus the pebbles, versus the sand in their busy lives and to shake things around a bit to make room to volunteer some time and talent to help our pack and their son realize the promise of Scouting. We hope you will be willing to do this too."

There is a second story or skit that I have used to make an impression on potential pack volunteers. This also makes an effective Cubmaster Minute, where you can also ask some of the Scouts to assist you.

Start with a cash register tape that is very long—the longer the better. Use this tape to represent the lifeline of a Cub Scout in your pack—no need to name someone. Place highly visible markings at equal intervals across the tape, numbered from 0 to 90. Have a Scout hold one end of the tape and another Scout hold the other end so the entire tape is visible to your audience. You're ready to deliver your message...

"Folks, this tape represent the lifeline of one of our Scouts. I would like to spend a moment to explore the times in their lives when as adults; we can make the highest impact in their lives that they will remember."

Walk from the low numbers to the high numbers of the tape, saying "At the far end of the tape—we can all acknowledge that it is our hope that as adults, our kids outlive us".

Tear off any of the tape beyond the number 65, and allow the Scout to let it drop to the floor as he now holds the tape at the number 65.

Walk back towards the low numbers on the tape and share, "Of course—who among us can truly recall those early years, when our parents fed us, changed our diapers and taught us how to talk?" Tear off any of the tape before the age of 6, and allow the Scout to let it drop to the floor as he now holds the tape up at the number 7.

Next say, "Once our kids reach college age—they tend to move out for school or careers. We really don't get to see them nearly as often from this point on—as we do now." Tear off any of the tape beyond the number 18, and allow the Scout to let it drop to the floor as he now holds the tape at the number 18.

"In some families, once kids reach their teenage years—it can be challenging to find ways to stay connected with our kids. They develop relationships out of the home, explore new interests—in short, it may no longer be as cool to hang with mom or dad or the family." Tear off any of the tape beyond the number 12, take both ends of the remaining tape from the Scouts and raise it up for the audience to see.

"As you can see—it turns out that the years your son is in Cub Scouts are the ones that they will be the most receptive for you to make an impact in their lives that they will remember. Our pack can use your help on a task or two to make this experience memorable and impactful for all our kids. Please see us right after the meeting and we can tell you how."

I have never seen these stories not produce at least one volunteer from the most reluctant crowd.

Lastly, consider this… if you're not having fun, you're doing it wrong. To the degree you can make volunteering a fun thing for adults to do—an assignment they look forward to because of fellowship—if not content, the more tasks and roles your pack adults will willingly accept.

We will cover some of the dynamics of developing an effective team of volunteers and how to run meetings that respect people's time in a later chapter. After all—both of these elements will be necessary to do well if you are to build a stronger pack—your Scouts will love—in only an hour a week. But before we move on from the topic developing volunteers—let's spend a moment to explore adult recognition.

Let it be established that the primary focus on recognition in Scouting is for the youth. Given this priority, it is also important to note that Scouting developed recognition programs for adult volunteers as well—so you might as well utilize them to the advantage of your volunteers and pack.

There is unit level and individual level recognition that may apply to your volunteers. One of the first forms of volunteer recognition that can be earned is the "Trained" patch. I always monitored volunteer progress towards fulfilling these requirements carefully—taking time at roundtables, den meetings and pack meetings to call out the achievement in a brief ceremony and to explain how it is important to the Scouts and the pack.

One reason to do this is I wanted to acknowledge that a volunteer took the extra time and effort to earn the distinction—as an expression of their passion to serve our Scouts well. I thought it might also be important for the Scouts and families to understand that their pack leaders were taking the time to learn a new role and that learning was an important life-long habit.

Another common individual adult recognition is the Scouter Training Key—which acknowledge the completion of all required formal training along with some tenure in serving the specific role. At one time, there were specific awards for Tiger Cub den leader, Cub Scout den leader, Webelos Scout den leader, Cubmaster, committee chair and pack committee member. At the time of this writing, these role specific awards are planned to be consolidated into the Scouter key, starting in January 2014.

Going forward, should you wish to demonstrate repeating the earning of the Scouter key—you would add a Scouting device (a small pin representing Cub Scouts, Boy Scouts, Venturing, Exploring or commissioning) to the existing knot. Knots are the Scouting term for such recognition patches.

If you have a longer tenured Cubmaster—they may be eligible for the unit leader award of merit. In addition to a unique knot design, this recognition also includes a Cubmaster patch with a star added to the design. (A similar award is available for Scoutmasters and Venturing crew advisors.)

There are several other adult knots that a leader may wear on their uniform. Whenever our pack held a joining event or spoke with prospective pack families, I always made it a point to explain why volunteer leader uniform insignia should be important toward their decision to join our pack. The same was true for unit earned recognition.

If you ask your unit commissioner or district executive, they can also let you know about recognition you can award your non-registered adults in the pack. You don't need to be wearing a Scout leader uniform to be recognized for your contribution to Scouting.

There are several unit level recognitions available to your pack as well. I include them in this section because I believe the receipt of such recognition can be satisfying and meaningful feedback for your volunteer leaders that they are doing a terrific job and making a meaningful difference with their time commitment to your pack. Unit recognition can include banners for the pack flag, recognition pins (i.e. summertime pack) and quality unit award pins and patches.

The quality unit awards are especially interesting. The latest program (Journey to Excellence or JTE) provides feedback to your pack regarding the strength of your pack program against a national standard or benchmark. You now have the means to judge the effectiveness of your program against any pack in the U.S.A. Prior to the JTE, you could only speculate how the quality of your pack program might measure up to others. The exciting news about JTE is that it can guide you when creating your annual pack program plan—and throughout the year—so your unit can earn the level you desire.

Your unit commissioner can not only provide you deeper insights and guidance about JTE, they are standing by to help you connect with any of the district or council resources you need to achieve the JTE score your unit desires to earn. You can also get more information about adult awards and devices from your unit commissioner.

If you really want the success of your pack to continue after you have moved on to other opportunities in Scouting (troop, crew, district or council roles), you should also consider your depth chart or succession plan for pack volunteers. Packs are notorious for cycling between large and small membership levels and stronger and weaker program. The most consistent packs avoid this cycling by using a succession plan to assure a continuation of leadership experience.

It is worth mentioning that it can be a challenge to accurately predict your next leader. It has been my experience that some individuals destined for leadership greatness never truly step forward to fulfill this potential. Likewise, sometimes the individual who just doesn't seem to have leader charisma or deep talent—winds up being an indispensable leader for your pack. My advice—try not to pick your next leaders, let them pick you by their actions.

The way to do this is to pay attention to this year's leader roles and then look forward a year or two. You will obviously need den leaders, a Cubmaster and a committee chair. Less obvious might be the person that will run next year's pinewood derby. This year, your pack might have the pinewood derby expert for the whole district. She may have been running the derby for your pack, with flawless execution for 3 or 4 years now. Looking ahead, her youngest son is now an Arrow of Light Scout and will be crossing over to join his two brothers in their troop. Perhaps this might be a good year for her to mentor another volunteer to pass on the pinewood derby secrets for the following year—when she plans to be an active volunteer in the troop versus the pack. It pays to consider these scenarios and prepare. After-all, you don't want to wait until you are thirsty to begin digging a well.

Every pack should have at least one BALOO trained leader, but frankly, the more leaders who have BALOO training—the stronger your pack program will be. The same can be said for your Webelos Scout den leaders and the OWL course (Webelos Leader Outdoor Training). Ask your unit commissioner about these important advanced leader courses for pack volunteers. I think you will learn, as I did, that having a steady stream of your pack leaders taking these course, every year, is one of the best decisions you can make towards building a stronger pack—your Scouts will love—in only an hour a week. Then again, without a succession plan, you may never see a gap in pack volunteers who have the benefit of taking these courses until it is too late to help you on an outing.

The Medieval Castle—located at Camp Cutler, in Naples, New York

Chapter 7

Program Ideas

Make no mistake, it is important for Scouting's success that Scouts have fun. After all, it was Scouting's founder—Baden-Powell—who said, "Scouting is a game with a purpose". Equally important is to recall that Scouting is also not merely a craft club or activity session. Through the delivery of our Scouting program, Scouts will find a fun way to explore new things, grow and become good citizens and future leaders. It is games with a purpose.

Our challenge is to keep it interesting and fun for the Scouts. Your question might be, "how can we learn how to do this?" I thought I might share with you some of the sources we have learned to use to help make Scouting fun.

As I mentioned in prior chapters, Scouting has created den and pack meeting plans. These plans layout in a page or two, all the tasks and supplies needed to conduct a successful meeting. There are sufficient plans created to support a den meeting each week of the year and a pack meeting every month of the year. There are far more meeting plans to choose from than the average den or pack will require in a year. The advantage of the incremental plans is it provides the option to select different meeting plans each year to keep things fresh. While the plans are already different for Bear Scout dens vs. Wolf Scout dens—extra plans also means that next year's Wolf Scout den(s) do not need to repeat the same activities and sequence as this year's Wolf Scout den(s).

Oddly enough, a second excellent source of program is the contents found in the Cub Scout handbooks. Our pack learned to review all of the achievements needed for rank advancement, as well as for arrow points. We always wanted to keep our gathering activities for our den and pack meetings fresh (after all, how many crossword puzzles or word searches do you want to fill out to start a meeting?) We learned that a secret to an effective meeting was to have a gathering activity at the start of each meeting that captured the Scout's attention. Since not all the Scouts arrived at the same time, the gathering activity gave Scouts something to focus on while we waited for the last Scout to join us. Without the gathering activity, we found that all of our Scouts youthful energy channeled itself into behaviors that made it nearly impossible to rein them back into order when the formal meeting was ready to begin. Once we learned the power of using gathering activities—our meetings and our advancement smoothed out quite nicely. This also makes it easier to find and keep den leaders.

By using these rank advancement activities during den and pack meetings, we found we had a great source of variety to choose from, while at the same time, helping the Scouts progress towards more recognition.

Another consideration when selecting content for a den or pack meeting is the overall energy level for the meeting. If the main activity burns up a lot of energy, the gathering activity may want to be a quieter selection. If the main activity will be quieter, do yourself a favor and begin the meeting with a gathering activity designed to consume some of their youthful energy. Some Scouting topics can be on the quieter side—let's try to avoid approaching them so passively that the Scouts are having flashbacks of their afternoon Social Studies class. Once you have selected the topics for a meeting—ask yourself how it might be presented creatively and with energetic fun. Guest speaker? Skit? Go-See-It? Consider your options...

In my experience, the strength of your pack is dependent upon the strength of your dens. Strong dens are the result of two primary ingredients: fun program and fellowship.

Generally speaking, boys like to play with other boys. If den size is small, due to low recruiting success or low attendance—you will have challenges keeping your dens strong. When boys know that their friends will be at the meeting, they will want to be there also.

The most relevant and influential leader for Cub Scouts is the den leader. If your den leaders can get into the practice of personally contacting Scouts to encourage them to attend meetings and pack events—you will see high recruitment and retention numbers for your pack. If you simply send an e-mail saying "we hope to see you there" you will find your attendance to be highly variable. Imagine the impact on a boy to get a call from an adult, whose opinion they respect like that of their den leader, who shares with them how important it is that the Scout be at the event and that it won't be the same without them. It raises their self-esteem and also encourages a sense of responsibility for supporting the team. These are qualities we wish to promote and nourish.

I know that when we had a pack event, there was more effort involved to personally arrange and contact members of the pack to encourage and confirm that they would be there. The result was a strong and growing pack with a tremendous sense of belonging on the part of our pack families. When only an e-mail reminder was used to promote events—participation would drop off rather dramatically. People don't care how much you know—unless they know how much you care. Let your Scouts and pack families know how important it is for them to be a part of your events and you will see your pack morale and numbers soar.

Your program selection and delivery determines the interest and fun your Scouts will have, but it also creates and paces the recognition that they will receive. The pack meeting is where each of the dens can describe for others the activities they have shared as well as be recognized for the achievements they have earned. Given this—be aware to plan a steady stream of achievement that can be recognized at each pack meeting so that all your pack families will be motivated to attend. If the den is in-between achievements, plan ahead so that Scouts can earn a pack level achievement.

Further to this point, carefully consider the method you will use for recognition. Whenever possible, include both the Scout and their family in this ceremony. Vary the ceremonies that you use to keep things fresh. Make sure you are not simply handing a Scout a new patch—do something to make the moment special and memorable.

There are many sources for recognition ceremony ideas. Some examples follow:

We built an advancement ladder, where each rung on the ladder represented a rank in Cub Scouts. We took old neckerchiefs and wrapped one for each rank around a different rung on the ladder, allowing the lower tip to hang down so the rank was displayed. A Scouts name was written on a clothespin. We used a highlighter pen to match the clothespin color to the current year rank. As a Scout advanced in rank, they physically moved the clothespin from rung to rung. Their first rung was Bobcat—up to Arrow of Light. Sounds basic, but physically moving yourself up the rungs—along with your family members, seemed very tangible and meaningful to both the Scouts and their families. Imagine the image of all the clothespins representing the Scouts from your pack displayed on your pack ladder! This is especially impactful when you have year round recruiting.

Another approach is to purchase the glow in the dark sticks. When you snap them to make them glow in the dark—you break a small divider inside the stick that allows two chemicals to mix to make the glowing color. If you carefully cut the opposite ends of the stick, you can separate the chemicals yourself. Place one chemical in a small container, like a baby food jar. Give a baby food jar containing this chemical to each of your Scouts to hold during their recognition ceremony. Keep the other chemical in a separate jar that you hold, along with a small dropper. As you progress down the line of recognition expectant Scouts—you can ask them an easy question about Scouting or their achievement. Let them, and the audience, know that if their answer is true, the color in their jar will change when you add a drop from your jar (naturally, your choice of questions can never have a wrong answer). It adds a nice bit of showmanship to the meeting.

I have also read about a technique where you can soak the neckerchiefs in a solution so that you can set them aflame, but they will not burn. In a ceremony where a Scout receives their neckerchief, this might be quite impressive! I bring up this particular technique to make a point. I am not particularly gifted at performing magic tricks—although I can appreciate their attraction to Cub Scouts. Recognizing my limitations in this area—I chose not to incorporate this ceremony into a pack meeting. I rationalized my decision by convincing myself that it might not demonstrate for the Scouts a respect for fire. You do what you have to do...

Depending on where you are located, you may have roundtables and/or pow wows that you can attend to get additional program ideas. These are incremental training opportunities for you and your pack leaders to gain additional skills and ideas for Scouting. Since Scouting has been around awhile, if you search on-line on E-Bay, Scouter blogs, LinkedIn Groups, and the various sites I will mention in a later chapter on valuable resources—you will find volumes of materials and ideas from various Councils, capturing prior content shared at past Scouter training events. In many cases, these ideas can be purchased very inexpensively—if not easily obtained (quite legally) for free. They are a great way of re-discovering tried and true program ideas all over again.

Speaking of roundtables—you should definitely promote attending your district's roundtables and council training events amongst your pack leaders. If they are new to packs—or simply new to their current role in the pack— they will be grateful you suggested they go when they find answers to many of their questions. They will further benefit from the positive association and fellowship they will find there from their peers.

If they are experienced Scouters, they may be pleased to learn that others will value the experience they could share with the lesser tenured leaders. Many a Scouter has found that sharing their hard won knowledge with an enthusiastic crowd at roundtable breathes fresh energy and passion into their personal Scouting experience. There is no telling how many people that may be positively affected by this. Offer to car pool the group to roundtable. The more members of your pack that attend roundtable, the stronger your pack program will become. If you're not careful, you may find yourself forming lasting friendships with like-minded, exceptional adults in the process.

If you speak with your unit commissioner, they can help you to identify other opportunities to learn program ideas through resources that are available within your district or council. You will find that when a pack leader attends a BALOO course, they will return with both new ideas and new energy to serve your pack. Likewise, I have never failed to see a den leader return from taking the OWL course (Webelos Leader Outdoor Training) who didn't have a bounty of new ideas to share with the pack to the benefit of your Scouts. If these course names are unfamiliar to you—see your unit commissioner, they will fill in the blanks on what they are and why you will not want to miss them.

I was very fortunate, early in my adult Scouting experience. I showed up to receive my Cubmaster specific training on a training weekend and happened upon two pieces of information that I would not have heard about otherwise. I feel they made a big difference towards the success of our pack.

The first thing I learned was there was a monthly meeting, called a roundtable, where Scout leaders shared tips on how to do Scouting. I was thrilled to learn that I was qualified to attend. Turns out, our pack routinely held our pack committee meetings on the very same night as roundtable. I might never have heard about roundtable if it were not for attending that training. Long story short, because I insisted I needed to be at roundtable, we ultimately changed our pack committee meeting night and several members of our pack started to come to roundtable with me.

My second stroke of good luck at training was I learned about another Scouting course called Wood Badge. For adult leaders, the world of Scouting today centers around making improvements through teams of volunteers. With this in mind, Scouting has developed an advanced course to help leaders learn how to construct a vision for how to make Scouting better, and then plan and execute the realization of that vision—generally through collaborative teams of Scout volunteers.

The course content is so impactful and so impressive, that many companies will pay for their employees to take the course. The good news is—you qualify to take this course. In my case, I was just starting out in Scouting as a leader. I knew by taking the course at the start of my Scouting experience, that I would gain knowledge, skills and contacts from the course that I could then apply to my Scouting efforts from the outset.

Does Wood Badge work? It depends on your measure of success. In my case, I took the course concurrent with accepting responsibility to Cubmaster a pack of about a dozen actively attending Scouts. At best, our pack committee meetings involved four people at the time (2 of which were moving up to troops). In two years, we grew pack membership to 60 Scouts, we had two trained den leaders per den, over 90% of our pack families played a supporting role in the pack, we qualified annually for quality unit and we averaged over 90% of our Webelos Scouts crossing over to troops—almost all as Arrow of Light Scouts. Our pack committee meetings grew to over fifteen regularly attending members. Wouldn't you like that kind of help for your pack? If your goal is to build a stronger pack—that your Scouts will love—in only an hour a week, this kind of broad engagement is how you do it in the hour a week part. I credit much of this success to the lessons I learned and the projects I defined to work on while taking the Wood Badge course.

Most people I know already feel like their plate is full. The average individual may advise you that now is not the best time to add to your plate with a course like Wood Badge. I need to tell you that for yourself and for your desire to make Scouting better for someone dear to you—you cannot afford to not to take the course. Just by deciding that you will go, you will be amazed how other obstacles that you perceived would block your progress will fall away or become resolved. Typically, if your only blocker for taking the course is financial—your council will have a solution for this. Take Wood Badge—there will be no regrets.

To find out more about the Wood Badge course, have your unit commissioner introduce you to someone who has completed the course at your district's next roundtable. You will not be disappointed.

Chapter 8

Running a Pack

One of the key ingredients to building a stronger pack—your Scouts will love—in only an hour a week is to make volunteering as easy as possible for members of your pack. This chapter will focus on some topics that might help you to do this more effectively.

The Scouting model heavily relies on our ability as volunteers to come together to work collaboratively towards a common cause of Scouting. We manage to do this despite a fantastic diversity of backgrounds, talents, biases and lifetime experiences. I hope that in your pack, this process of volunteers coming together and working effectively as a team seems simple and straightforward. In the event this is not always the case—it may be important for you to know that this is perfectly normal.

In the mid-1960s, Bruce Tuckman authored a theory on group development that you may find useful for Scouting (or any other group you may be a part of). His theory supports that a group experiences a performance progression across a multiple of definable stages of development. Being aware of this phenomenon can be helpful to put group behaviors you experience into some kind of context.

The first phase a new group experiences (or sometimes when an established group faces a significant new challenge) is the Forming stage. During the Forming stage:

- The group is busy with new routines: who, what, when, etc...
- Group members want to be accepted by the others, so they tend to avoid controversy or conflict.
- Group members gather information and impressions about each other and the group's purpose and how to achieve it.

Groups mature from the Forming stage to the Storming stage where:

- Ideas compete for attention.
- Group members begin to define goals and what leadership they will accept.
- Interactions are more open and candid (occasionally bordering on confrontational—hence the Storming stage).

Most of the time (but not always), the group will progress from the Storming stage to the Norming stage where:

- The group focuses on a single plan for their work.
- Individual ideas are incorporated or laid aside in a spirit of cooperation.
- The group is acting as a cohesive whole with a sense of ambition and shared responsibility.

The rate of maturity from stage to stage can greatly depend upon the experience of the leader to help the group move through the stages, as well as the combined social maturity, emotional quotient (EQ) and skill of the group members. As a result, the timeframe to move from stage to stage can vary by group. Occasionally, groups can fall back a stage or two with the introduction of a significant number of new group members or when a significant new challenge is thrust upon them, throwing the performance of the group off its "A" game. One can only imagine the impact on a pack committee when experienced leaders cross-over (exit) with their sons to troops in the spring, while a new group or Tiger Cub parents enter the pack in the late spring and fall.

Recognizing you may be moving through this group development dynamic can sometimes be helpful towards better understanding where you are and where you are going. I thought it might also be important for your sanity to share that occasional group dysfunction is a normal part of the process. It is mentioned here to facilitate that benefit.

Another aspect of working with teams is the realization that we don't all process the same information in the same way. If you are already well attuned to this reality—accept the possibility that others in your group are less enlightened. Scouting develops the adults, as well as the Scouts...

Many years ago, a trusted mentor recommended that I read a book to better understand why others respond differently than I to information or circumstances. I found the book to be very helpful towards learning to work with others in a way that was more compatible to how they respond to the world. The book, written by Florence Littauer, is titled, "Personality Plus". I strongly recommend it.

The premise of the book is based on four personality types. While no person is a pure type, most of us have a dominant type, with a lesser blend of the others. All types have distinct patterns and strengths—which when taken to an extreme could also represent a potential weakness. While an initial bias may be to form a group of all the same type—I have found a clear advantage in my Scouting (and professional) experiences to value the diversity of the various personality types, since they all can contribute in their unique way to a stronger group—or for our purposes, a stronger pack your Scouts will love.

One of the four types is called the choleric—they are the natural born leaders who will fill any vacuum in leadership. At their best, they are decisive, driven, sure. To an extreme, they can become a bit dogmatic and autocratic (bossy?)—driving for action and becoming impatient with discussion.

Another personality type is the sanguine. They are the life of the party and make the process fun. You definitely want to have some sanguine types amongst your pack leaders. One aspect of a sanguine personality to be aware of is that they also tend to be less structured by nature. Left unsupported by your other personality type leaders, the sanguine Cubmaster will deliver a very fun pack meeting—but it is unlikely it will ever start or end on time, or cover all the intended content. An understanding of personality types can help you be aware of this possibility so your pack can compensate for this—if this is important to you (if it is important to you—you are not a sanguine).

A third personality type is the phlegmatic. This is the unflappable, steady leader in your pack. The great part about a phlegmatic is that if they agree to do something, you can count on it getting done. The part you may have to compensate for is that a phlegmatic will complete the task on their own timetable and terms and generally do not like being micro-managed or pushed (then again, who does?).

The fourth personality type is the melancholy. People with strong melancholy tendencies can be either very analytical, very creative or both. What a wonderful asset to have when planning an important pack event! One of the quirks many melancholy personalities can exhibit is they can be highly sensitive (moody?).

To over-simplify, if you are going to have a pack event where the choleric leads a plan, drafted by the melancholy to include a lot of fun activities suggested by the sanguine, where the preparation is carried out by the phlegmatic—things are going to work out fine. Shift everyone over one chair and the results could be less certain.

I have learned that being aware of these types of patterns when working with a group of volunteers can be very helpful. My intention was not to manipulate the group, based on these traits, but rather to better understand how they process information and communication and to find more effective ways to work with each of them in a language or approach they were more receptive to. This also helps the team transition faster and with more certainty through the Forming, Storming, Norming and Performing stages.

Personally, I am a choleric, with melancholy tendencies—possessing almost no sanguine or phlegmatic traits. I am an analytical organizer and can be prone to a decent creative thought now and then. My greatest gift may have been that I can create a sense of confidence in what we were trying to do as a pack so that other adults are inspired to volunteer to be a part of it. I am also aware that making a game fun for boys is not my strongest suit. However, our pack was blessed to have a leader (a sanguine) who was fantastic at making things fun. By following my plan, but using his delivery—we more than tripled the membership in our pack through stronger program. It didn't hurt that our sure and steady (phlegmatic) den leaders built a strong sense of loyalty and belonging in our Scouts—delivering regular advancement goals that we could recognize each month at our pack meetings.

This was simply a smart way of leveraging the combined strengths of our leaders. We were ultimately able to get over 90% of pack adults engaged at some level in the delivery of program in our pack in some form or other—each of them bringing their own strength to the mix. In my opinion—this is what valuing diversity is all about, but to get there, it helps to have some awareness as to how people tick.

I would like to add a final observation with regards to personality type. Personally, my reward is getting things done. However, I am also aware that for some people—it is also very important to take a moment to celebrate the victory. Since I seem to possess a genetic flaw that inhibits me from stopping to embrace the win (a very choleric viewpoint—after all, the next goal awaits…), I have come to recognize (through hard won self-awareness of my EQ) that when working with more diverse groups—it is an important part of the process to celebrate achievement. I have learned to compensate by always having someone on the committee (likely a sanguine) who pays attention to group celebrations. This is yet another example of how awareness of personalities and what makes people tick allows you to build a stronger team.

Since I brought up the term micro-manage earlier; let's talk about this aspect of working with a team. Across my professional as well as volunteer leadership experience—I have witnessed three leadership approaches: Deploy & Hope, Command & Control and High-Performance. In spite of ourselves, most of us shift from one approach to another as we lead a team—but as the names might suggest, one of these approaches far outperforms the others.

The Deploy & Hope approach occurs when an assignment is poorly defined and there is little follow-up during the delivery of the task. Frequently, there is no objectively measureable description of what the successful delivery of the task would look like, no clear understanding of the resources available, no clear understanding of decision-making authority and no prior agreement regarding the nature or frequency of status updates. Under this style, it is often difficult to even know when the task is finished! The trouble with doing nothing is knowing when you're finished...

Imagine being asked to plan the blue & gold celebration for your pack. Now imagine the same assignment where you are yet to experience a blue & gold yourself, are not informed as to who should be invited, have not been told what budget limits or personal spending authority you may have or whether or not someone will even ask you another question until the day of the event. Having fun yet?

To some degree, the opposite of Deploy & Hope is Command & Control. In this approach, even the tiniest detail of the assignment has already been scripted and seemingly every progress step on every task must be reported—in real time. No true decision-rights are granted in this model, since all decisions, no matter how small, must be pre-approved. In the end, it appears as though the volunteer's help is not really needed, if only the person "in charge" would have the time to do it all themselves. Feeling valued or trusted?

So what would the High Performance approach look like? Imagine if we took the time to draft some objectives for our blue & gold ceremony:

- We wish to invite all of our Scouts and their families
- Members of our Chartered Organization should be invited

- We would like members of our Scout district to attend
- We intend to hold a cross over ceremony for our departing Arrow of Light Scouts—as they transition to their troops
- We would like representatives from each of the troops receiving our Scouts to play a part
- We would like each Scout to earn and be presented their badge of rank at the blue & gold
- All dens will be given a role to play during the event to display their talent and entertain our guests
- We would like to serve refreshments and use event related decorations
- We would like the event to last 90 minutes
- We have a budget of $300, which the blue & gold chair can spend—providing there are receipts for expenditures submitted to the Treasurer
- The blue & gold chair can work with the Cubmaster regarding program content details and timeframes
- We will start planning 3 months in advance and review progress as a part of our monthly pack committee meeting

If you were the next blue & gold chair for your pack—which approach would you prefer to work with? So would your pack volunteers.

It takes a little more time to establish the high performance approach—but believe me—compared to the other two approaches, the time invested is well worth it. When applying it to someone less experienced, simply break down the steps a little smaller and decrease the time between check-ins to be a little shorter. As you both gain experience and confidence working together, you can broaden the tasks and lengthen the periods between status reports. This avoids micro-managing, as well as Deploy & Hope. Try it, you will be amazed at the capabilities you will see developed in others when you do...

Speaking of pack committee meetings... If you wish to respect your volunteers and their limited time, always try to have an agenda for your meetings (den, pack and pack committee) which are distributed ahead of time so folks can prepare. I always shared a copy of the pack meeting plan with every member of our pack leadership who I was calling upon to play a role. As you can imagine, things never flowed exactly per the plan, however, because we all had a plan and better understood who would play what role, in what sequence and approximately for what timeframe—it always made adapting to unexpected changes (or opportunities) a lot easier.

We always published a pack committee meeting agenda in advance of the meeting. This helped us to travel through the items on schedule so that folks could return home to resume all the other things that fill their day. The agenda also helped reduce the wave of last minute topics that can sometimes be introduced and can make the meeting drag. We set a goal to publish notes from the meeting within a day or so—since we found that a written record of what was agreed to allowed people to move forward confidently on assigned tasks with pre-knowledge about important deadlines. Too often, meeting notes are published from the last meeting, just prior to the next meeting. Volunteers have very busy lives—anything we can do to make their role in Scouting easier is a big plus—and happy pack families tell their friends about Scouting.

One way to keep planning and communication simple is to create a planning and tracking table (you can do this electronically in MS Word or Excel). In the example that follows, you will see entries are organized by topics in the columns and by month in the rows. The columns would be based on the structure of your pack committee. In addition to documenting the den and pack meeting content—other pack functions or initiatives can be captured as well, such as membership, popcorn, special events, re-chartering, ...

If you create this table during your annual program plan, it won't take too much time each pack committee meeting to more deeply explore the next 3-4 months, drop the prior month and potentially add a month or two as it comes up on your pack radar. We have found a similar format useful at a district and council level as well. There is no reason a document like this could not be shared with your pack families. Keep in mind, it can be a relatively dynamic document—so you will need to keep distributed copies current or folks may actually be misinformed about your plans.

71

Pack Service Plan

Mo	Theme	Tiger Den Plan	Wolf Den Plan	Bear Den Plan	Webelos Den Plan	Arrow of Light Den Plan	Pack Plan	Events	Join Scouts	Pop Corn
Sep	Courage	# 1,2,3 Go-See-It	# 2,3,4	# 1,2,3	# 1,2,3	# 1,2,3	# 1,2,3	Hike	School 1	Show n Sell
Oct	Respect	# 2,3,4 Go-See-It	# 6,8,5	# 2,3,4	# 2,3,4	# 2,3,4	# 2,3,4	Camp	School 2	Show n Sell
Nov	Honesty	# 5,7,8 Go-See-It	# 9,7,10	# 5,6,7	# 5,6,7	# 7,8,9	# 5,7,8	Food Drive	Church A	Take Order
...	...	...	...	...	...	...	...			

One of the challenges of communicating with pack members is how do you effectively reach everyone? In our ever increasingly busy world, how do we share a concise and efficient way to exchange information, and to be able to tell whether this information has actually been successfully received?

I would like to tell you that if you create an accurate contact list for the families of your pack—you can simply send out an e-mail and be certain everyone has received it and will be coming to your pack event. Sadly, I have not found this efficient solution to be particularly effective. In addition to e-mails, we have also tried Facebook and a pack website. Assuming the website administrators are vigilant at keeping all the information contained there up to date—the truth is, even this slightly more modern method is still one one-way communication

Our pack has attempted to use a website or Facebook page to share information. This can be useful for posting pictures, contact information, schedules (the pack service plan), etc... The shortcoming of the website/Facebook approach is that it is not ideal for gathering important feedback from pack members. While it lets you push information out, it is not effective in conveying how important your Scouts are to you as a leader, or for them to feel the personal encouragement from their Scout leader to be at the next event. This is a bigger shortcoming than you may know. If you do use a website or Facebook page—this doesn't mean you should stop. Just be aware that other aspects of your communication with people will need to be addressed through other methods.

My advice is to leverage the natural strength within your pack—your dens. Realistically, the strongest connection between your families and your pack is their den and den leader. Assuming your dens are the typical size of 6-8 Scouts—this makes for a reasonable "phone tree" whatever the actual method of contact. The important part of this method is the two-way exchange of information. Your den leader, the leader the Scouts and adults are most connected to, makes a personal contact promoting the next meeting or event and seeks some confirmation that the den member will be there. This also creates the opportunity to reinforce how important it is to the den that the Scout is there. Everyone likes to know that people look forward to them coming and that the event will not be as much fun if they are not there. This vital personal contact accomplishes two things for the pack. It builds stronger program by encouraging more members of the den or pack to attend the event—and it provides feedback, in advance of the event, regarding intended participation. I'm afraid merely sending out a tweet or e-mail blast that says "we hope to see you at the park, Saturday" is a poor substitute. If you take the time to reach out to your Scouts in this personal way—there is no telling what kind of an impact you may have in their lives. It may all have started because an adult they look up to cared enough to call to make sure they would be joining in with the rest of the den.

This last statement reminds me of a terrific Cubmaster minute that goes something like this:

> Draw the Scouts near so you can show them an apple and then split it in half so they can see the seeds in the one half of the apple.

> Glance at each Scout and then say, "it is a rather simple thing to determine how many seeds are in an apple".

> Pause a moment and then finish, "but, it is a greater challenge to know how many apples are in a seed".

"It is similarly a challenge for us to know, as Scouts, how many people will someday benefit from one of our good deeds".

Make sure you make brief eye contact with a pack adult you have been trying to get to volunteer for a role in the pack... See that adult after the meeting.

Author playing at Wood Badge
Not an official BSA publication and the BSA is not responsible for its content

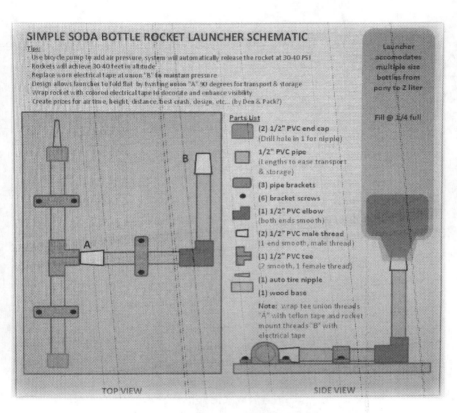

SIMPLE SODA BOTTLE ROCKET LAUNCHER SCHEMATIC

Tips:
- Use bicycle pump to add air pressure, system will automatically release the rocket at 30-40 PSI
- Rockets will achieve 30-40 feet in altitude
- Replace worn electrical tape at union "B" to maintain pressure
- Design allows launcher to fold flat by twisting union "A" 90 degrees for transport & storage
- Wrap rocket with colored electrical tape to decorate and enhance visibility
- Create prizes for air time, height, distance, best crash, design, etc... (by Den & Pack?)

Launcher accomodates multiple size bottles from pony to 2 liter

Fill @ 1/4 full

Parts List

(2) 1/2" PVC end cap (Drill hole in 1 for nipple)

1/2" PVC pipe (Lengths to ease transport & storage)

(3) pipe brackets

(6) bracket screws

(1) 1/2" PVC elbow (both ends smooth)

(2) 1/2" PVC male thread (1 end smooth, male thread)

(1) 1/2" PVC tee (2 smooth, 1 female thread)

(1) auto tire nipple

(1) wood base

Note: wrap tee union threads "A" with teflon tape and rocket mount threads "B" with electrical tape

TOP VIEW

SIDE VIEW

Just add water, bicycle pump, bottles and Scouts …

Chapter 9

Valuable Resources

The wonderful thing about Scouting is that there is a world of Scouters who wish to share their knowledge and passion for Scouting with you. Given this, I thought I would share some of the sources you could explore for more information, in addition to the ones I have shared in previous chapters.

For starters, we should mention the obvious. **Scouting.org** is a treasure trove of information that can meet your Scouting needs. The materials, tools, applications and information that you can find on this website can keep you busy for hours, if not days.

A couple of observations may be helpful. The Boy Scouts of America is acutely aware that their website is slow and difficult to navigate. Now, you know this too. The best work around is to Google the topic of interest, because it will deliver for you an easy link to access the topic within the Scouting. org site. This tactic works great and will save you both the frustration of conducting searches from within the Scouting website itself or the wait times for the website to finish processing your query. Since this tactic essentially solves the key problem when using the Scouting.org site, be happy the BSA is devoting funds and attention to other aspects of Scouting that have less elegant work-arounds. The quality of the materials on this site is excellent— once you can find them, so make sure you check this site regularly, so when something new is added your pack can be the beneficiary.

There are a few additional sites I would like to bring to your attention.

One of the most impressive is **ScoutmasterCG.com**. Although the site may appear on first blush to be primarily intended to serve volunteers in the Boy Scout program (whereas your primary focus is Cub Scouts), I have found this site—created and managed by Clarke Green—to offer outstanding advice regarding the intended spirit of using program to develop youth within the Boy Scouting movement. I would make it a daily habit—you will value insights and content shared on this site long before your son has reached the age to cross over to a troop. When I grow up, I want to gain the wisdom and talent I have witnessed in Clarke Green—he must be a special leader.

For Cub Scout program specific content there may not be a better site than **Baloo's Bugle**—which can be found at **usscouts.org**. Make this site a regular stop each month and your pack will never run out of fresh and interesting material to use so that you can build a stronger pack—your Scouts will Love—in only an hour a week. Here is an additional secret you can share with other Scouters—there are numerous back issues ...

I found the following sites very useful towards deepening my understanding of Scouting, and for providing incredible program ideas to add fun and variety to our pack and den meetings. They are a great source of free information, but many also feature products well worth considering investing in for the benefit of yourself—if not your pack...

http://www.boyscouttrail.com a terrific, unofficial source of Scouting information and program ideas

http://www.scouter.com another great site for unofficial Scouting information and program ideas. This site also features Scouter blogs by topic matter.

http://www.cyberbasetradingpost.com website providing products for purchase and program ideas for conducting campfires, ceremonies and award presentations. It is very helpful for building strong pack program. Our pack, district and council events have benefitted from the use of an indoor campfire—originating from this site. You will want one too.

http://www.cub-roundtable.com/ not only does this site contain a wealth of incredible ideas you can use for skits, songs, games, ceremonies—it also contains convenient links to multiple related sites. Great program ideas you Scouts will love—free of charge!

http://www.macscouter.com/ part of the US Scouting Service Project, MacScouter is a prime destination for program ideas and tips—including pow wow books. This is incredible material that will add fun and variety to your pack program—all free of charge.

http://boyslife.org/ if your pack does not have <u>every</u> Scout receiving their very own copy of Boys' Life magazine every month, you are doing your Scouts and your program a disservice. What boy wouldn't be thrilled to arrive home from school to discover they have received something in the mail. Written to appeal to Scout age youth—the material shared in this magazine will help keep your boy's excited about Scouting (and reading).

http://insanescouter.com/index.php another amazing site where you can find free Scouting tips, Scouter blogs and products for sale that you will want to know about, in order to build stronger program that your Scouts will love.

http://kismif.org/ while this site is no longer being updated, it is still a great source of Scouting advice, web links and products that you will want to be aware of.

http://www.netwoods.com/scout_links.html this is an excellent site to consult in order to find out about, and obtain links to the constantly growing number of web sites containing valuable information about Scouting and Scouting activities.

http://www.scoutingthenet.com/ this site contains almost 2,000 links to great Scouting program ideas and information.

http://thetrainerscorner.wordpress.com/ a series of Cub Scout leader helps and posts including topic categories like program fun, leader helps, Scouting outdoors, Webelos-to-Scout, and more…

http://www.inquiry.net/toc.htm pages and pages of ideas and links for program content you will not want to miss.

http://www.thedump.scoutscan.com/nonfict.html Warning: The material contained in this website may improve your Scouting program!

http://www.scoutmastercg.com/ this has become one of my very favorite sources of Scouting content and sage advice. This site offers the option of email updates for new content. You will want to take advantage of this. The Scouter blog is administered by Clarke Green, a very capable and experienced Scouting volunteer. This site will be of interest to you in whatever capacity you may serve in Scouting. I recommend daily reading.

http://www.scouting.org/ the official website and content for the Boy Scouts of America. The content is very high caliber, but at present, the site can be challenging to navigate or search for the content you desire. Don't let yourself be a victim of circumstances. If you Google the topics of interest, Google will provide you the link to the content you seek on this site. Problem solved. Check this site often since content is updated frequently. Well, well, well worth any trouble.

Chapter 10

Helpful Cub Scout Terms

A

aims of Scouting They are character development, citizenship training, and mental and physical fitness.

Akela (Pronounced Ah-KAY-la.) A title of respect used in Cub Scouting—any good leader is Akela. Akela is also the leader and guide for Cub Scouts on the Wolf trail. The name comes from Rudyard Kipling's Jungle Book. See "Law of the Pack."

Arrow of Light Award The highest rank in Cub Scouting and the only Cub Scout badge that may be worn on the Boy Scout uniform.

Arrow Point An award for earning 10 elective credits as a Wolf or Bear Cub Scout: The first 10 electives earned in either rank are represented by a Gold Arrow Point; subsequent groups of 10 earn Silver Arrow Points.

Arrowman A youth or adult member of the Order of the Arrow.

B

Baden-Powell, Robert Stephenson Smyth The founder of the worldwide Scouting movement. He was born in London on February 22, 1857, and was made a baron in 1929. He is referred to as Lord Baden-Powell of Gilwell, Chief Scout of the World. He died January 8, 1941.

BALOO (Basic Adult Leader Outdoor Orientation) This training experience teaches volunteer leaders how to plan and carry out an outdoor experience for Cub Scouts.

belt loop See "Cub Scout Academics and Sports program."

blue and gold banquet A birthday dinner for Scouting held by Cub Scout packs in February to celebrate the founding of the Boy Scouts of America in 1910 and of Cub Scouting in 1930. May be called "blue and gold dinner."

Boy Scout A registered youth member of a Boy Scout troop or one registered as a Lone Boy Scout. On second reference or in informal usage, "Scout" is synonymous with "Boy Scout." The Boy Scout badge signifies fulfillment of the joining requirements; it does not represent a rank. See "Boy Scouting."

Boy Scouting That part of the program of the Boy Scouts of America for boys and young men not yet 18 years old, and who are at least 11, or have completed the fifth grade and are at least 10 years old, or who have earned the Arrow of Light Award in Cub Scouting and are at least 10 years old. Boy Scouts advance through Tenderfoot, Second Class, First Class, Star, and Life ranks to Eagle Scout. The emphasis is on outdoor activity, learning skills, developing leadership ability, and service. The unit is a Boy Scout troop. See "Scouting program."

Boy Scouts of America The legal name of the organization is singular. The abbreviation is BSA (without periods) and is used with the article ("the BSA") when used as a noun. See "National Council" and "national office."

Boys' Life The magazine for all boys published by the Boy Scouts of America.

C

charter In the BSA, charters authorize (1) an organization to operate BSA Scouting units (see "chartered organization"); (2) a local council to incorporate as a BSA local council; (3) operation of an Order of the Arrow lodge; or (4) the Boy Scouts of America to incorporate. See "Charter of the Boy Scouts of America" and "Charter and Bylaws of the Boy Scouts of America.

chartered organization A religious, civic, fraternal, educational, or other community-based organization that has applied for and received a charter to operate a BSA Scouting unit.

chartered organization representative A manager of Scouting in a chartered organization who also represents this organization in the local council and district.

commissioner A commissioned Scouter who works with packs, troops, teams, and crews to help units succeed.

council An administrative body chartered to be responsible for Scouting in a designated geographic territory.

crew (1) A working group of Sea Scouts in a ship. There are usually several crews in a ship. This compares with the Cub Scout den, the Boy Scout patrol, and the Varsity Scout team. (2) A working group of five to 12 members of a high-adventure base contingent.

Cub Scout A registered youth member of a Cub Scout pack or one registered as a Lone Cub Scout who has completed first grade but who has not yet completed third grade, or who is age 8 or 9. See "Cub Scouting."

Cub Scout Academics and Sports program A supplemental enrichment program that complements Cub Scouting. A pack may select any of a multiple of sports or academic subjects to pursue. Academics or Sports belt loops, pins, and jacket letters recognize the Cub Scouts for participation and practice.

Cub Scouting That part of the program of the Boy Scouts of America for boys who are in the first grade through fifth grade (or are 7 through 10 years old). Tiger Cubs are in the first grade (or age 7); Cub Scouts, second or third grade (or ages 8 or 9); and Webelos Scouts, fourth and fifth grade (or age 10). The unit is a Cub Scout pack and the pack is made up of dens of the various age groups. The emphasis is on family-centered activities, group activities, learning, and having fun.

Cubmaster A volunteer Scouter, 21 or older, appointed by the chartered organization to lead a Cub Scout pack.

D

den A neighborhood group of six to eight Cub Scouts or Webelos Scouts that meets periodically, usually once a week, and is part of a Cub Scout pack.

den leader A volunteer leader, 21 or older, appointed by the pack committee to plan and direct the den's activities.

district A geographical area of the council determined by the council executive board to help ensure the growth and success of Scouting units within the district's territory.

district committee the district committee coordinates the functions of the district to carry out the policies and objectives of the council. The executive officer of the district committee is the district chairman.

district executive A professional Scouter who works under the direction of the local council Scout executive and acts as an adviser to the volunteer leaders in the district.

E

executive board The executive board in each local council is its policy-making body. Voting members include between 25 and 50 regular council members, the chairmen of the committees of the executive board, the chairmen of the district committees, and up to two youth members. The Scout executive is a nonvoting member.

F

Friends of Scouting (FOS) Use this term instead of "Sustaining Membership Enrollment." An annual opportunity for Scouters and interested people in the community to be identified with the local council through their financial support and influence in the expansion of the council program.

G

Good Turn for America A national service initiative by the BSA to address the issues of hunger, homelessness, and poor health. Participating organizations include the American Red Cross, Habitat for Humanity, and The Salvation Army.

I

immediate recognition patch This Cub Scout patch indicates how Cub Scouts are progressing in rank. As a Cub Scout fulfills requirements, he earns the Progress Toward Ranks beads, which hang from a leather thong attached to the pocket button.

J

Journey to Excellence Scouting's Journey to Excellence is the performance measurement and recognition program for councils, districts, and units that replaced the Centennial Quality program in 2011.

L

Leave No Trace The BSA is committed to this nationally recognized outdoor skills and ethics awareness program to reduce impacts on the environment and other people. The seven principles should be followed at all times in the outdoors: Plan ahead and prepare; travel and camp on durable surfaces; dispose of waste properly (pack it in, pack it out); leave what you find; minimize campfire impacts; respect wildlife; and be considerate of other visitors.

local council An administrative body chartered by the National Council to be responsible for Scouting in a designated geographic territory. Voting membership may include active members at large and chartered organization representatives. The program is directed by an executive board of volunteers and administered by a Scout executive and staff of professional Scouters.

M

methods of Scouting The eight methods are the ideals (Scout Oath, Scout Law, Scout motto, and Scout slogan), patrol method, outdoors, advancement, association with adults, personal growth, leadership development, and the uniform.

N

National Council This is the corporate membership chartered by the United States Congress to operate the program of the Boy Scouts of America. Members include all elected members of the National Executive Board, members of regional executive committees, elected local council representatives, elected members at large, and elected (nonvoting) honorary members. The program of the National Council is directed by the National Executive Board and administered by the Chief Scout Executive and a staff of professional Scouters at the national office and in other locations.

O

Order of the Arrow Scouting's national honor society. Youth members must hold First Class Scout rank; they are elected by all youth members of the troop, based on their Scouting spirit and camping ability. The aim of the OA is to promote the outdoor program and service to Scouting.

P

pack A group made up of several Tiger Cub, Cub Scout, and Webelos Scout dens. The pack includes not only the boys in the dens but also their families and leaders.

parent and family talent survey An inventory of parents' interests and abilities conducted by the Cub Scout pack to determine program potential.

pinewood derby A pack activity that involves making and racing small wooden cars on a track.

pow wow A one-day training conference for Cub Scout leaders.

professional Scouter A registered, salaried, full-time employee who is commissioned to serve in an approved professional position in a local council or on the national staff by having successfully completed formal training.

Q

Quality awards Replaced by the Centennial Quality Award until the end of 2010. Recognition given each charter year to units and each calendar year to districts, councils, areas, and regions that commit to and meet specified national standards pertaining to leader training, service, advancement, camping, and membership growth.

R

raingutter regatta A pack activity that involves making and racing model boats.

rank The six Cub Scout ranks are Bobcat, Tiger Cub, Wolf, Bear, Webelos, and Arrow of Light Award. There are six ranks for Boy Scouts and Varsity Scouts: Tenderfoot, Second Class, First Class, Star, Life, and Eagle Scout. The Sea Scouting ranks are Apprentice, Ordinary, Able, and Quartermaster. Combinations: "First Class rank," "Star Scout."

registered member Annually, every youth and adult who wants to join or continue membership in the Boy Scouts of America must submit a completed application form or reregister and pay an annual registration fee. Membership is a privilege, not a right.

religious emblems program Various religious organizations have designed requirements and procedures for participants in this Scouting program to earn the religious emblem of their faith.

Religious Principle, Declaration of The Boy Scouts of America maintains that no person can grow into the best kind of citizen without recognizing an obligation to God and, therefore, acknowledges the religious element in the development of youth members. However, the BSA is absolutely nonsectarian in its attitude toward that religious development. Its policy is that the organization or institution with which youth members are connected shall give definite attention to their religious life. Only adults willing to subscribe to this declaration of principle and the Bylaws of the Boy Scouts of America shall be entitled to certificates of leadership.

roundtable An event conducted by a roundtable commissioner and roundtable staff to help the unit leadership of a district plan and carry out their own unit programs.

S

School Night for Scouting A one-night event held in a neighborhood school, place of worship, community center, etc., where boys and parents gather to hear how Cub Scouting and Boy Scouting operate and how they can join.

Scout reservation or camp Land owned by or leased to the Boy Scouts of America to further the Scouting program. A Scout reservation usually has two or more camps.

Scout shop A BSA-owned store, operated by the Supply Group, that sells official Scouting merchandise.

Scouter A registered adult member of the Boy Scouts of America who serves in a volunteer or professional capacity.

Scouting Anniversary Day February 8, 1910, was the day William D. Boyce incorporated the Boy Scouts of America.

Scouting movement An idea started in England by Baden-Powell, based on the conviction that boys can live up to a code of conduct and can develop themselves physically, mentally, and spiritually in association with other boys through a program of appealing activities and advancement challenges under the guidance of adults.

Scouting.org Official website of the Boy Scouts of America. The website provides resources and information about Scouting for youth, parents, volunteers, alumni, and the general public.

Scouting program Historically, "Scouting" has been the generic term for the organization and activities of the Boy Scouts of America. It refers also to Boy Scout, Varsity Scout, and troop and team activities. The program of the Boy Scouts of America is designed to fulfill its chartered purpose to achieve objectives in character development, citizenship training, and fitness adapted to the age groups: Tiger Cubs, Cub Scouts, Webelos Scouts, Boy

Scouts, Varsity Scouts, and Venturers. The program is carried out in units run by local organizations chartered by the Boy Scouts of America.

service center The business office for a local council.

Silver Beaver Award A recognition given by the National Court of Honor for distinguished service to youth within the council.

space derby A pack activity that involves making and racing model spaceships.

square knot Generally, embroidered square knots are representative of pin-on medals or around-the-neck awards and are designed for the greater convenience of the wearer. Embroidered knots from other Scout associations may be worn on Scouters' uniforms.

T

Tiger Cub A boy who is in the first grade (or is 7 years old) and registered, with his adult partner, as a member of a Tiger Cub den.

Tiger Cub den A den of five to eight Tiger Cubs and their adult partners. Part of a Cub Scout pack.

trained leader Every leadership position in Scouting has several training requirements to be considered fully trained. When a leader completes all of the requirements for the particular position, they are qualified to wear the "trained" emblem on that uniform.

Trained Leader emblem This emblem may be worn by all leaders, youth and adult, who have completed the Fast Start and basic training programs appropriate to their positions. It may be worn only in connection with the emblem of office for which training has been completed.

troop The unit that conducts Boy Scouting for the chartered organization.

U

unit The entity that conducts Scouting for the chartered organization; it consists of registered youth members and registered adult volunteer members. A unit may be a pack, troop, team, crew, or ship. Its affairs are administered by the unit committee, which is appointed by the chartered organization.

unit leader The adult leader of a unit is a Cubmaster, Scoutmaster, Coach, Advisor, or Skipper.

V

Venturer A registered youth member of a Venturing crew. The word "Venturer" should be used only as a noun referring to a youth member.

Venturing The young adult program of the Boy Scouts of America for men and women ages 14 through 20, or 13 with completion of the eighth grade.

Venturing crew Youth members and adult leaders who conduct the Venturing program within an organization chartered by the BSA.

W

Webelos badge The fifth rank in Cub Scouting; earned by Webelos Scouts in a Webelos den.

Webelos den A group of Webelos Scouts who meet weekly under the supervision of a Webelos den leader.

Webelos den leader A registered volunteer member, age 21 or older, appointed by the pack committee to plan and direct the den's activities.

Webelos Leader Outdoor Training A supplemental training experience conducted by the district or council to provide Webelos leaders with the skills needed to conduct den parent-son overnight camping.

Webelos Scout (Pronounced WEE-buh-los.) A Cub Scout who has completed the third grade or is age 10 but has not yet completed fifth grade or reached age 11 1/2, and is a member of a Webelos den. The word "Webelos" (means WE'll BE LOyal Scouts) should always be used as a modifier, never as a noun.

Webelos Scout overnighter A one- or two-night campout by Webelos Scouts and their adult partners.

Webelos-to-Scout transition plan When Webelos Scouts become Boy Scouts. The preparation and graduation of a Webelos Scout from Cub Scouting to Boy Scouting.

Wood Badge Training award granted upon completion of the Wood Badge for the 21st Century course. A leather thong with two wooden beads, a special neckerchief, and a slide (woggle) are worn by those who have completed the training.

Y

Youth Protection program This BSA emphasis fights child abuse by teaching youth the "three R's": Recognize, Resist and Report child abuse; by helping parents and Scouters learn to recognize indications of child abuse and situations that could lead to potential abuse; and by teaching them how to handle child abuse situations or reports.

Chapter 11

Keeping in Touch ...

I am not well practiced on social media. Facebook seems like a lot of work and frankly, while I have an account—I have no idea how twitter works or what I might tweet that the world needs to read about right this moment.

I do recognize that the fellowship shared amongst Scouters is a very powerful thing. In the event you have read this book and would like to follow-up with a question about an idea, share your own idea for others to try or simply stay connected with other thought-leaders within the Scouting world—I encourage you to connect with me at www.fortheloveofcubscouts.com

I welcome your feedback about the book. I would love to hear back from you regarding any ideas you would wish to share such as:

- Recruiting Cub Scouts
- Retaining Cub Scouts
- Successful Webelos transitions
- How to get pack adults to volunteer
- Fund raising ideas
- How to get pack families excited about fund raising
- Program ideas to try with your pack

I will do my best to continue to explore and share additional helpful links, materials (like the soda bottle rocket launcher plans) and fresh ideas on Packs not contained in this book. More importantly, by sharing your ideas on this site, I hope we can all benefit from the broader world of Scouting and the positive learning of others dedicated to its continued success.

Sometimes, someone else has already found the words to express what you would like to say in closing. This might be one of those times. I wish you the very best in your quest to build a stronger pack—your Scouts will love—in only an hour a week. I am humbled that you selected this book in an effort to gain some further insights into how you might accomplish this. It is my fondest hope that you found something of value here. I would leave you with this passage from Scouting's founder—Baden Powell...

I believe that God put us in this jolly world to be happy and enjoy life. Happiness does not come from being rich, nor merely being successful in your career, nor by self-indulgence...

But the real way to get happiness is by giving out happiness to other people. Try and leave this world a little better than you found it and when your turn comes to die, you can die happy in feeling that at any rate you have not wasted your time but have done your best. "Be Prepared" in this way, to live happy and to die happy—stick to your Scout Promise always—even after you have ceased to be a boy—and God help you to do it.

Your friend,

Baden Powell of Gilwell

Josh as a Arrow of Light Scout
Not an official BSA publication and the BSA is not responsible for its content